HANSEN

HOBBLE CREEK PRESS
An Imprint of Cedar Fort, Inc.
Springville, Utah

To Louise B. Hansen, who raised me on homemade bread

ISBN 13: 978-1-59955-973-5

Published by Hobble Creek Press, an imprint of Cedar Fort, Inc.
2373 W. 700 S., Springville, UT 84663
Distributed by Cedar Fort, Inc., www.cedarfort.com

LIBRARY OF CONGRESS CATALOGING-IN-PUBLICATION DATA

Hansen, Mark (Rulon Mark)
 Dutch oven breads / Mark Hansen.
    pages cm
 Includes index.
 ISBN 978-1-59955-973-5
 1. Bread. 2. Dutch oven cooking. I. Title.
 TX769.H274 2013
 641.81'5--dc23
                              2013027886

Cover design by Erica Dixon
Cover design © 2013 by Lyle Mortimer
Edited and typeset by Casey J. Winters

10 9 8 7 6 5 4 3 2 1

Contents

Introduction
The Magic

"Cooking is art,
Baking is science,
Baking bread is magic."

I DON'T know who said that first (and I've done some research), but I believe it! As I started learning how to cook in a Dutch oven many years ago, baking presented me with a particularly difficult challenge. Which surprised me, actually. My first attempts were quite successful. The very first thing I ever cooked in my new Dutch oven was pizza. After only a year of doing stews and meats, I did rolls for a cook-off, and they turned out great!

But the first loaf of bread I tried was a disaster. It didn't rise well and ended up looking like, and frankly tasting like, a doorstop. The first time I tried an apple pie was even worse. I had problems keeping the coals lit, and in the end, the filling ended up more like applesauce. It was horrible.

Dutch oven baking, for me, was like this: the more I tried and the more I learned, the worse it got!

I tried all kinds of bread recipes. I tried to get the right blend of ingredients to make it light and tender and not like a brick. Some of my efforts were passable, others even bordered on good, but I never felt like I was really "getting it right." I kept feeling like I didn't have the *magic*. My mom and sister could cook great bread, why couldn't I? Maybe the mojo skipped me.

I finally realized that part of my problem was the cookbooks. Too many of them were simply a list of ingredients and sketchy outlines of instructions. Cooking is so much more. The process is critical, especially in baking. It was as if the cookbooks assumed I already knew what they were trying to teach me. Well, that doesn't do me a whole lot of good, now, does it?

I got some good help from my mom and sister, and in the process, I got a few really good breadmaking books. I learned how to knead and for how long. I learned what flours to use and how long to store them. I learned about the core ingredients and about enrichments. I learned about gluten and how to coax it out of your flour and into your bread. As I practiced all of these things in my Dutch ovens, I learned about heat management and how to preheat the Dutch oven.

Then I learned about quick breads and chemical leavens. I learned about cookies and cakes and how to make pie crusts and fillings.

I found a lot of help in books and from lots of good people. But one thing that frustrated me was the scarcity of comprehensive books on baking bread in a Dutch oven using coals. It seemed to me that there should be more. Baking bread is a part of every Dutch oven cook-off. And every cook-off has delicious entries, in many different types and styles. Many Dutch oven cookbooks have bread recipes in them, but bread isn't their focus. There are few definitive how-to guides on baking bread in a Dutch oven.

Now, I don't know how "definitive" this book will be. I don't claim to be an expert baker. The readers of my blog who have followed along for all these years will certainly attest to that! But, over the years, I've used my blog to share my learning and my own growth. Those same readers can see the progress, and I've shared my newest insights with them as I've discovered them. I hope to be able to share a bit of the magic with you.

Lifting up the lid of your Dutch oven to see and smell your fully baked loaf truly is a magical moment. You turn it out onto the cooling rack, and you can see the golden brown crust, and the aroma swirls around you. It's almost intoxicating. And finally, after a time, you get to bite into it and taste the joy.

Baking bread *is* magic.

HOW TO USE THIS BOOK

Some of you will have come to this book because you want to learn how to make great bread in your Dutch oven, and you've had a tough time figuring that out up to now. If that's why you're here, that's great! I would recommend that you start from chapter one. It's designed for you to have some quick success, with an easy loaf of no-knead artisan hearth bread.

Then, move on to chapter two and bake a delicious loaf of kneaded bread. These two chapters are written and designed with enough instruction that you can do them easily and correctly and get consistent results each time.

After you've made these loaves a time or two, take some time to read through chapter three. Here you'll find some of the real details of bread baking. You'll see how to do it and why it works. You'll learn about the right tools, the right processes, and the right ingredients. Finally, you'll be ready to tackle any of the recipes in the rest of the book.

Others of you might have gotten this book because you feel pretty confident in your bread baking and you simply want to find some new ideas and some new recipes. For you, the best way to use this book is to pick a recipe from chapter four and beyond. Each recipe contains sufficient instructions to pull it off with distinction!

Later, if you're so inclined, you can go back through chapter three and learn a lot of the details and processes. With that knowledge kneaded into your head, you'll be able to invent and create your own breads and your own unique recipes.

In whatever case, I hope you find lots to try and lots to taste!

ASSUMPTIONS

We all know that making assumptions will get you into trouble. It will. It's just a matter of time.

Still, in spite of this, I need to make a few assumptions. I'll ask you to make them along with me so we can be working on the same page, so to speak.

First, I'm going to assume that, as the reader, you have a little bit of experience cooking in a Dutch oven. Maybe you've made a few dump cake cobblers and maybe a stew or a chili or two. And I'm going to assume that you've done these things outdoors using coals. That can be on your back porch or out camping in the woods or mountains. If you've done a few things in a Dutch oven before, this book will make much more sense.

If you are brand-new to the wonderful hobby of Dutch oven cooking, welcome! I would recommend getting a little bit of experience before taking on this book. One of my other books, *Black Pot for Beginners*, is an excellent primer. If you've gone through that book, you'll be able to deal with this book's instructions with ease.

I will explain these recipes step-by-step and as completely, simply, and clearly as possible. Even so, I would still recommend a bit of experience first. Baking isn't easy. Baking in a Dutch oven, because of all the variables, is even trickier.

In this book I won't be talking about how to season Dutch ovens, how to take care of them, or what kind of ovens to buy. I'm going to assume you're aware of those things. Instead, I'm going to focus on baking bread.

Second, I've adapted many of the recipe procedures for circumstances that are not common in the typical kitchen—one of the most obvious is avoiding the use of electrical appliances.

My wife razzes me about this constantly. I'll be making a cake and struggling with mashing butter and sugar into a creamy froth using a slotted spoon or a potato masher, and she'll casually say, "We paid good money for a mixer, you know?" or, "This wonderful device has attachments for breadmaking!"

These recipes and instructions will, for the most part, not use these appliances, for several reasons.

The first reason is that I want people to be able to use these recipes in different circumstances. On a wilderness campout, for example, you won't have a power outlet or a way to carry in a big mixer. But you may still want to cook up something delicious and impressive.

Also, I really like the feel of the bread dough in my hands as I knead it. I can tell when I've got the right amount of flour and when I'm done with the kneading all by the feel. Using a breadmaker takes that away from me.

As of this writing, the current rules for the International Dutch Oven Society (IDOS) World Championship Cook-off prohibit the use of electrical appliances. As a result, most of the smaller, regional cook-offs (which are often qualifiers for the big WCCO) also prohibit their use. Now, not everyone is going to compete on a world-class level, or even in a city or regional level, but if someone reading this book wanted to use one of these recipes in a cook-off, I'd like for them to be able to do that without a lot of changes.

The second reason I avoid appliances is I feel that it connects me a bit more historically to my ancestors who used the Dutch oven to cross the great American plains and then as they carved out a living in the Utah desert. My life is quite different from theirs, but I like to feel a bit connected to them as I cook.

So if you want to use a blender, a mixer, or a whatsamawhosit-thingamajig that you happen to have in your kitchen, by all means go ahead. You should be able to adapt everything and make it work just fine. I won't judge. On the other hand, if you find yourself outdoors without a power outlet or you simply wanna go retro, then you can! This book will help you either way.

Third, some people will say that it's best to do your baking using regular bread pans or pie tins placed in a Dutch oven. They say that it's easier to clean, easier to remove, or it's a more typical shape for the final product.

That's all true, and all well and good, but I'm going to bake directly in the Dutch oven. That's my assumption. Partly for IDOS rules and partly because I just wanna. If you manage your heat correctly, you won't burn the bottom. If you use a parchment lifter, you can pull your corn bread out. Or you can serve it "directly from the Dutch."

I'm also assuming that not everyone will read this book from start to finish. I hope people will read the beginning chapters. I've written them with the intent that they be informative, and they provide a lot of the knowledge base that's so valuable to moving forward. The other sections of the book are essentially recipes drawn from the entries of my blog, Mark's Black Pot.

The point of this assumption is that a lot of things may get repeated, particularly in the processes of the recipes. This is because some people will simply look up particular recipes, and I want them to be able to do a good job without having read the previous pages of the book.

Finally, I don't make the assumption that I'm right or that I'm the final authority—I'm just sharing things that I've learned. People have been making bread and biscuits for many hundreds of years, and everyone's grandma does it differently. People have been using Dutch ovens for many, many years, and we all do it in our own little unique way. But I hope you find something useful and practical in my books, and if it helps you make a great birthday cake or a really amazing loaf of artisan bread, then you and I have both accomplished something great!

THE ROMANCE AND SPIRIT OF BREAD BAKING

I love a lot of things about breadmaking, and especially about doing it by hand.

When I cook a chicken or a roast, I can work with it. I can season it, cut it, marinate it, sear it, braise it, or whatever else I want to do with it. But it's really still a dead hunk of meat.

The vegetables I cook with are, technically, still alive when I'm working with them, but they're on their way out. I mean, they've been cut from their roots and their nutritional sources. We put them in the fridge or in bags to help keep them from dying off faster, but from the moment they get cut off at the farm, it's almost over for them. It's a dead celery walking, and I'm the executioner, with a chef's knife instead of a guillotine.

Besides, they're not growing or anything. They're, well . . . you know . . . vegetables.

On the other hand, a boule of bread dough is a living, breathing colony of life. Up until the moment I put it in the oven, it's feeding, growing, thriving. And that's not simply a casual side effect of the breadmaking process—it *is* the breadmaking process. Without yeast bugs eating, reproducing, growing, and burping out CO_2, we would have no leaven and we would end up with a brick.

Even before we fully understood the nature and origin of germs, we've been using yeast from the air to make our breads fluffy. In the Gospel of Luke, "leaven" was used to describe how the saints would spread the joy of the gospel. For centuries since then, bread has been used in sacraments to remind disciples of the principles of Christianity.

Sometimes I like to think about all that while I'm kneading a big ball of dough under my fingers. Other times, I'm just thinking about the dough. In either case, I feel it being squashed and stretched between my fingers, and I love the sticky coolness. Gradually, with a little motion and a bit more flour, it becomes more elastic and holds its shape more and more. Then, I know that as I set it aside it will breathe deep and grow in the rising. I'll punch it down and beat it up as I shape it, but it will grow back, and finally, in the heat of the oven, it will swell up to a full loaf and set its shape, with a rich brown crust and a light and fluffy crumb.

Then I get to eat it!

THE NEED FOR PRACTICE

THE 2 PERCENT

I wanna tell you a couple of stories about learning how to bake good bread. The first one happened after I had been struggling for a while to get a really good loaf of bread going. I was talking with my sister, who is an incredible chef and a wonderful bread baker (though she doesn't do Dutch ovens). She had just given me some advice, and we had been talking about some ideas to make my Dutch oven breads work better.

Then she commented to me something along these lines:

Some people who occasionally make bread want to do it quick and fast, or they are happy to just have a loaf that will make their house smell great every other month or two. Maybe they'll try a new, fast recipe that they've recently read about in a magazine or online. They're pretty much happy with whatever comes out of their oven. That's about 98 percent of home bread bakers.

But the other 2 percent want to learn how to make the crumb as light and airy as possible, and they want the crust to be perfect—brown and crunchy. These bakers are always trying to bake bread better, and they are never quite fully satisfied until they can produce amazing results every time.

After a short breath, she said, "Mark, welcome to the 2 percent!"

That was a major boost to my confidence. I knew that no matter what, I would eventually be able to produce the kind of loaves I wanted to, over and over again.

I also knew that the more I did it, the more I would learn. And the more I would learn, the pickier I would become and the higher my standards would be.

I also knew that it would take some practice. Baking bread in a Dutch oven is a different experience. I'm going to try my best to share with you the benefit of my experience, but that can't fully substitute for your own experience. The more you bake in a Dutch oven, the more you'll learn about how much to knead and how many coals to use, and when and if you should replenish them. You'll learn how much heat you'll need to make the bottom crust soft and not burned.

How good you are matters less than how much you're trying! Over and over and over again!

Now I get to say it to you: Welcome to the 2 percent!

THE BREAD PARTY

I like to show off.

A few years ago, as I was finally getting to the point in my baking experience where I felt some real confidence in my abilities, I hosted a bread party. It was kind of an experiment, but one that worked out well.

I planned it out for some time in advance. I invited the guests and thought carefully about the breads I would prepare.

I began the preparations weeks before the event, catching a wild yeast culture and working it up into a great sourdough starter. I baked some of the loaves a few days before because I knew I would only have enough time to do a couple of loaves on the day of the party.

The day of the event, I served up, if I recall correctly, five or six full loaves of different breads. A sweet sandwich loaf, a sourdough, a rye, a whole wheat, and a few others I don't remember. I served cold cuts and cheese for sand-wiches, and I made a cheese fondue in my 8-inch Dutch oven.

The party was fantastic. All of the guests tried various kinds of breads, and all were filled. It was quite an accomplishment for me, because, as I mentioned, I had struggled so long to learn the magic of Dutch oven breadmaking. It was, for me, a landmark in my progress as a Dutch oven chef.

Will you need to host such an event? Not necessarily. But, if you follow the steps in this book, it's my hope that you'll feel that kind of confidence.

THE INTERCONNECTEDNESS OF ALL THINGS

Even though this book is all about doing breads, and even though it focuses mostly on yeast breads, I noticed something as I wrote. The more I cooked and the more I learned, I started to realize how closely related all of baking is. Think about it: you take some core, simple ingredients, and the end result really is only a difference of a few elements.

For example, start with some kind of flour. Add a liquid. Add a leavening agent, like yeast, and you'll get a loaf of bread. Add enrichments like egg for structure and sugar for flavor, and it becomes even more rich and wonderful.

If you use a chemical leavener instead of yeast, like baking soda or baking powder, and omit the egg, you have biscuits or a soda bread. If you add the egg and some flavoring, like chocolate or lemon, you get a cake. Sometimes, we add bananas or zucchini to a cake and we call it a bread.

Lots of water or milk in your flour, and a chemical leaven, will give you a pancake batter. If you add less liquid, with a lot more butter and sugar, you'll get a cookie dough. Some cookie doughs are called "shortbreads."

If you use even less liquid and more fats (without leavening), you get a pie crust, which is a whole other game entirely!

Each of these recipes has its own tricks and techniques. Each is different in its own way. But they are similar at their core. The more I learned about each of these kinds of foods individually, the more I realized that this book needed to cover more. All of these things truly are connected. The more you learn about one food, the more you learn about another. And it's fun to cook them all in the Dutch oven.

So, while this book focuses on breads, mostly yeast breads, there is a section on chemical leavens. I hope you'll be able to see that connection as we go through the variations of all baking, and the big picture will bring it all together for you.

NO FEAR

After all of this blah blah blah and yadda yadda, the best advice I have to give you is this: Don't be afraid. Dive right in. Give it a try!

If you bake a few bricks along the way, it's not the end of the world. Forgive yourself and move on. Try again. Maybe you burned the top, or the bottom crust was too thick and dark. Maybe the middle was still doughy.

Oh well! Try again soon. We've all been there.

After all my talk of struggle, failure, and frustration, I hope I haven't scared you off. Enough with the talking. On to the baking!

Chapter 1
A Simple No-Knead French Loaf

LET'S TAKE Dutch oven breadmaking one step at a time. I put the following recipe here at the start so that someone just learning how to make breads in their Dutch oven can find quick and easy success. This will get you into the magic as quickly and easily as possible.

This first recipe is probably the simplest bread you will ever make. I'll take you through the process a bit at a time, explaining things along the way. In cooking, the process is as important as the ingredients. In bread baking, that's even more true. That's why I don't like most bread cookbooks. They have recipes with ingredients, but they're really short on process and instructions. I guess they assume you already know all that stuff.

Well, I won't follow such assumptions here!

No-Knead French Loaf

This recipe will take you two days, or one very long day. I don't mean you'll spend the whole day working on the bread, but from start to finish, it will be a long time. This is because we'll be doing a long, slow rise. We'll talk in more detail about yeast later, but what makes bread rise is the yeast gases getting trapped in the bread's gluten protein structure. Gluten is made when flour combines with water, over time. Kneading shortens that time, but to keep things simple and to develop more flavor, we're going to go with the long rise.

This kind of bread has been getting more and more attention in the breadmaking forums on the web in the last few years. Partly because it's simple, partly because it's delicious. I think it's a great opportunity to jump into breadmaking with some quick one-off success!

BASIC INGREDIENTS

Here's what you'll be starting with:

6 cups bread flour

1 tsp. active dry yeast

2½ tsp. salt

3¼ cups water

This is as basic as it gets. Eggs, oils, sugar, and other flavorings are just embellishments—enhancements to these basic four ingredients. You can add these enhancements to future loaves. But for this loaf, we're gonna stick with the basic four.

Let me say a few things about the flour. It should be bread flour, and it should be fresh. Yes, this can be done with all-purpose flour, but I wouldn't. I've had a lot of my bread loaves go south because I used old and/or all-purpose flour. Bread flour has more protein, so it can develop gluten better. We'll talk more about flours later on.

You can choose from many variations of yeast. You can get cakes of baker's yeast or little packets or little jars or whatever. This yeast doesn't need to be anything fancy. It doesn't have to be fast acting or anything else. We'll talk more about various kinds of yeasts, including wild-caught sourdough yeasts. But that's for a later chapter.

The salt is simply ordinary table salt. Its purpose is to enhance the flavor and to keep the yeast from going absolutely crazy in the bread.

For this recipe, since we're going to do a long rise in a fridge anyway, water temperature won't really matter, but I recommend using warm water if possible. In other recipes, the water temperature will be more critical. Also, if you're picky and you have access to it, filtered water is better. Straight tap water often has some chlorine, which can inhibit yeast growth.

BASIC TOOLS

In addition to the ingredients, you will also need these tools right away for the mixing:

Plastic or ceramic mixing bowl: I've read that some metals (particularly reactive metals like steel) can inhibit yeast growth. For that reason, I've adopted the habit of working with nonmetal materials. Plus, I find plastics easier to clean and carry anyway.

Wooden spoons: Wooden spoons are great for stirring. In this case, since this is a no-knead bread, we won't be stirring it up too much anyway, so it won't make a lot of difference. But I always keep a good, stout set of wooden spoons handy anyway.

1 cup measuring cup

1 teaspoon measuring spoon

You will need these tools for the prep and the baking:

Countertop or flat working surface: This can be your kitchen counter if you're indoors or a table if you're outdoors. It does need to be clean and solid so nothing falls through. If you're camping, you could even use a clean cutting board, if it's big enough. You will be doing some work on a floured counter, so you'll need to have that space.

Extra flour: This is to help you work with the dough.

Spray oil: You'll use spray oil to help you get the dough out of the bowl after the final rise. It's also the easiest way to coat the inside of your Dutch oven. (You could also dampen a paper towel with veggie oil and coat the inside.) By the way, baking bread is a great way to improve the patina coating of your Dutch ovens. Each time you bake bread, put on a thin layer of oil. The baking will add more to the coating!

12-inch shallow Dutch oven: Duh. This *is* a Dutch oven cookbook, after all. The oven should be well seasoned and, of course, clean. You can use a 10-inch and simply use a bit less dough, or you could also use a 12-inch deep and put a few more coals on top.

A leave-in thermometer that will measure up to 200 degrees F: I like the short-stemmed thermometers, but for some reason they're hard to find. When I do find them, I buy up lots of them. So many variables arise in Dutch oven cooking that it can be difficult to tell when the bread is done. Cooking to a particular temperature is the best way.

40 or more charcoal briquettes: Make sure you use a brand of charcoal that you've cooked with before and that you're accustomed to the "heat curve" they produce. You don't want sudden spikes or dips in heat when you're doing breads. Nice and steady is the way to go.

Matches, lighter fluid, or some other way of igniting the coals: Don't laugh. I can't count how many times I've forgotten this rather essential tool. It's embarrassing.

Dutch oven lid lifter: A lid lifter is an essential tool for all Dutch oven cooking. Choose the style you like, or you can even use pliers or a claw hammer.

Coal tongs: You'll want tongs so you can position and manipulate the coals. I like the longer ones, about a foot and a half. Never use your coal tongs to handle food, by the way.

Cooking surface for the Dutch oven: The cooking surface will vary depending on where you're cooking. Metal tables, a brick pad, hard-packed ground, even concrete can all work. Use common sense. Keep the heat away from brush or grass, and make sure that the area is well ventilated.

Gloves or hot pads: You'll be flipping the pot to get the bread out. That will hurt if you're doing it with your bare hands. Not a good idea. The bread itself will also be hot.

Cooling rack: As we'll see, the cooling is a vital part of the cooking process, not an incidental add-on. On a cooling rack, the air will surround the bread and will help to form the perfect bottom crust. Yum!

MIXING

Start by scooping up the six cups of flour into the mixing bowl. Different flours on different days will have different properties, and, as a result, will measure differently. To get a more accurate measure, don't pack the flour into the cup as you scoop. I like to scoop up the flour, hold the cup level, and shake off the excess, side-to-side. That keeps it pretty loose, and not tightly packed. Some will use the scoop and scrape method, where you use a butter knife to scrape off the excess flour. In my mind, if it was too packed to begin with, that wouldn't change anything.

Some measure the flour by weight. That's a good idea, because you'll always get the right amount, but I never have my scale handy, and most recipes aren't written that way either. In the end, you can adjust the amount to get the right consistency anyway.

I like to sift the flour too—not so much to get chunks out but more to aerate the flour and make it lighter. This isn't absolutely necessary, though.

Toss in the yeast and the salt. Since there's no liquid in there yet, they won't react. Stir them all together with your spoon or a whisk. Again, since there's going to be plenty of time for the yeast to get active, we're not going to "proof" the yeast in water first.

I said earlier that the water doesn't need to be warmed up, but I like to give the yeast every possible advantage, so, if it's possible, use very warm water. I once stuck a thermometer under a running tap so that I could tell what 110 degrees felt like. To me, it's like a hot shower and almost too hot. If you're out camping, you might not have a chance to heat up the water, so just use what ya got!

Pour in the water and stir up everything. Here's where you have to adjust the mixture to the right consistency. Add flour or water (at about a quarter cup at a time, or even less) to get it right. It should be runnier than a dough but more firm than a batter. It won't feel like normal bread dough, which pulls away from the side of the bowl as you stir. It will stick to the sides. It will hold together but not in a tight ball. If you shake the sides of the bowl, the center of the dough mass will jiggle. If you turned the bowl over, the dough would fall but not pour. It should be wet and gloopy, especially when compared to most bread dough you've ever worked with; however, it is not like a cake or pancake batter that pours and flows.

You don't need to stir it up too much. This process is not about kneading it to work up the gluten strands, but, rather, this is a matter of blending the ingredients. Once the dough is ready, set it aside to rise, still in the bowl and covered with plastic. Let it rise at room temperature for a while, even a couple of hours, until it's quite a bit bigger—this is to get the yeast active.

What if you're camping or outdoors or somewhere not room temperature? Yeast is most active at about 80 degrees Fahrenheit. What if it's 60 degrees out that day? No problem. Simply oil and flour one of your Dutch ovens and set it aside with 4 burning coals on the lid. That will heat it to about 80–90 degrees inside. If it's warmer outside, use fewer coals. Use more if it's colder, but not many more because you don't want to cook it. That's also why you don't want to put any coals underneath.

THE LONG (OVERNIGHT) RISE

This is the easy part: take the bowl and put it in the fridge. If you're camping and the dough isn't going to freeze overnight, simply leave the bowl out. Or if you mixed the dough in the morning and you're planning on cooking it 6–8 hours later in the afternoon, go ahead and use the fridge. The cool temperature will allow for slower fermentation, and the dough will rise, but not as fast. Otherwise, the yeast would run rampant through the flour and the dough would rise and collapse. Having the long ferment time will make the bread taste much richer too.

SHAPING, PROOFING

After the overnight rise in the fridge or the long rise in the afternoon, take the dough out of the cold and set it aside to warm up for a while, maybe as long as an hour. While you're waiting, get your cooking area ready and gather all of the tools you'll need for the baking.

Scatter a lot of extra flour around the work surface you're using (table, board, or whatever you've got), then dump the risen dough out onto it. It should flatten out a lot on its own because it's such a loose dough. Sprinkle more flour on top of the dough and put some on your hands.

Lift both sides up and fold them over onto each other, in thirds, like you would fold a letter. Let it flatten back out.

Turn the dough 90 degrees, and sprinkle more flour on top. Then stretch out the new sides and do the fold again. Turn it, sprinkle it, and fold it a third time.

This is really all the work you'll be doing with the dough. Again, you're not kneading it. It's really too runny to knead, anyway. But the fresh flour and the folding will redistribute and remix things a bit so the yeast has more flour to feast on.

Spray or coat the bottom and sides of the bowl fairly liberally with oil, and return the dough to the bowl. Set it aside (not in the cold fridge) for its final rise, which is called "proofing." In the picture below, I used a special cloth-lined proofing basket, which makes transferring the risen dough to the Dutch oven easier. But a well-oiled bowl works just fine.

BAKING

While the dough is proofing, it's time to get the Dutch oven ready. Start by lighting up 35–40 coals. The exact number isn't critical. Some of these will be used directly on the oven, while others will be a side fire to light coals for replenishing. While these coals are getting burned, stir them up occasionally so they're lit evenly.

Spray or wipe the inside of the Dutch oven with oil. You don't need much. If the Dutch oven is well seasoned, the oil probably won't stick much anyway, but it's good to make sure. Also, as the bread bakes, the oil will add to the black coating.

Set 10–12 coals in a circle under the Dutch oven, just underneath the edge of the bottom. Don't put them too far under—the heat will radiate inward, and putting coals too far under will create hot spots. For the same reason, spread 20–22 coals in a ring around the rim of the lid. Use more coals if it's windy or if it's cold out. If you're not sure, lean toward more coals on top and fewer underneath. For this kind of bread, though, hotter is better. You could go as high as 12 on the bottom and 24 on top.

Hold your hand about a foot above the Dutch oven and feel how hot it is. If you do that whenever you cook, you'll start to get a sense of how hot your ovens are, and you can better manage your coals.

Let the oven sit on and under these coals for at least 15 minutes. This will get the oven good and hot. Then, upend the dough bowl directly over the center of the Dutch oven. The dough will drop in and sizzle. If you have a sharp knife or a razor blade handy, cut a slice or two across the top. Quickly put the lid on the Dutch oven and mark the time. Putting the bread dough directly into a hot oven will make it "spring" and swell in the first minutes of baking. If the oven is really hot, it will help develop those large air bubbles that are so popular in artisan breads.

At this point, throw some fresh coals onto the remaining burning coals. These will catch and become your replenishers, if you need them. About 10 fresh ones should do.

The dough is now baking! In about 10 minutes, return to the oven and turn the lid about a quarter turn in any direction, using the lid lifter. Then lift the Dutch oven and turn it about a quarter turn, gently setting it back down. (Don't lift the lid during this process.) This will reposition the coals in relation to the bread baking inside—if there are any coals burning hotter than others, the heat gets redistributed.

After another 10 minutes, turn the Dutch oven and the lid again. This time, however, lift the lid briefly and check the bread. Look at the crust and see how brown it's getting. Here's the important part: stick a thermometer into the bread so that the sensor lead is in the middle of the dough. Reclose the lid as quickly as possible. The longer the lid is off, the more heat and steam escapes.

Tap the coals with your coal tongs to knock off the ash, which can insulate the coals and make it so less heat radiates. If it's been windy or the coals are burned down, replenish coals on the bottom or on the top as needed. Be careful with the bottom coals since it's very easy to overdo the under crust. Typically, if the lower coals are small and almost burned out, I'll put 3–4 fresh coals under the Dutch oven, just under the edge and evenly spaced from one another. Then I might add 4–5 coals on top. In most cases, however, if it hasn't been too windy, I will leave the coals as they are.

Finally, after another 10–15 minutes, the bread might be done. Lift the lid and check the thermometer. If the internal temperature is 180–200 degrees, then it's done! If it's not done, put the lid back on, turn it like before, and check it again in another 10–15 minutes. Remember to have the lid off as little as possible. Lift, check, close. If it's close to 180 or even just over, you could cook it a little longer. If you do, use only upper heat, to get additional browning on top!

If it's done, pull off the lid and take the oven off the coals. With the lid lifter, carry the Dutch oven to where you have your cooling racks waiting. Using the hot pads or gloves, gently turn the bread out of the Dutch oven. Then, still with the pads or gloves, turn the bread back over onto the cooling rack.

COOLING

When I first started baking bread, I didn't know any better and I would cut into the loaf almost as soon as it came out of the oven. I did this partly because I love hot bread. But mostly I did this because I wasn't sure if the bread was done, and I wanted to see. Unfortunately, it was usually not as done as I wanted. I didn't realize then that the cooling process is a part of the cooking process. The bread is still cooking as it's cooling. The structures are still setting. The smell will surround you and call to you. Be strong. Do not cut into it yet!

While you're waiting, you can clean out your Dutch oven. In all likelihood, there won't be much to clean. Typically, the oil and the black patina will have kept the bread from sticking, and it will need little more than wiping out. If there are crumbs inside, just rinse it out with hot water. After I bake, I like to re-coat it with a very fine layer of oil too, inside and out.

EATING

Once the loaf is cooled, cut it or tear it open. Take a good whiff of the aroma. As you bake more and more, you'll learn what it's supposed to smell like, and you'll be able to know when it worked well. Check out the crust. Is it browned, both on top and on the bottom? The top and bottom will look different, but they should both be done. Is it hard or soft? Look at the crumb (that's the body of the bread). Is it fluffy and a bit stretchy? That's the gluten. Are there air holes? Sometimes, you'll want to make bread with big air holes, and other times you'll want a tighter crumb structure. There should be some bubbles with this recipe.

Finally, give it a taste. All by itself, with nothing on it. No butter, no cheese, no jam. And let yourself really taste it. Roll it around on your palate. Get to know the flavor. The more bread you bake, the more you'll learn what you like and how the variations taste.

You can eat this kind of bread many different ways. I especially like to share it with friends, by simply breaking bread with them. Tear it in half and rip chunks off to share. Also, this is a great bread to have with butter and jam, or dipped in olive oil mixed with pepper and balsamic vinegar. It would go *great* with a nice hearty soup or stew! It can also be sliced, for sandwiches, but if there are too many holes in the crumb, or if the holes are too big, it won't really work for that as well.

CELEBRATING!

You've baked a successful loaf of bread! That's pretty exciting. Definitely worth celebrating. How did it turn out? How did it taste? How did it look and smell?

POSSIBLE PROBLEMS

Here are some bits of advice for troubleshooting possible problems:

Problem	What's Probably Wrong	What to Try Next Time
Doesn't rise as much	Yeast not very active	Maybe the dough didn't have enough time to rise and activate before it was put in the cooler. It might have not had enough time out of the cooler to warm up before it was shaped and proofed. It could be that it needed more additional flour and working in the shaping stage, to get more fresh food for the yeast bugs. If the flour was old, the gluten might not have developed to trap the yeast gases.
Doughy inside	Not done	Make sure that the tip of the thermometer sensor lead is in the center of the bread loaf so it can measure the temperature accurately. For that matter, make sure your thermometer is accurate. Keeping a good balance between bottom and top heat steadily throughout the cooking process can make a big difference. Also, make sure that the bread cools completely before eating.
Hard or burned bottom crust	Too much bottom heat, especially in the later stages of baking	Getting the proper balance between top and bottom heat comes with practice. When you replenish the bottom coals, don't put as many on, or wait longer to replenish.

Problem	What's Probably Wrong	What to Try Next Time
Burned top crust	Too much top heat, especially in the later stages of baking	When you replenish the top coals, don't put as many on, or wait longer to replenish. Also, don't leave top heat on as long, if you do that extended cooking at the end.
Not much "spring"	Oven not preheated enough	Put more coals on or wait longer for the preheat.
Heavy and dense, not light and fluffy	Not risen enough, or not enough heat	If the bread doesn't rise enough, it might not be getting enough gases trapped in the dough, so it doesn't expand in the oven. Also, if the oven isn't preheated or hot enough overall, then the gas that is trapped won't expand as much. Make sure that the dough is well risen and that the oven is good and hot.
Spots that are more brown than others	Uneven heat	Make sure that the coals are spaced in a ring fairly evenly both underneath the oven and on the lid above. Remember to turn the lid and Dutch oven every 10–15 minutes to prevent hot spots.
Bread is gone too quickly	You did a great job but didn't bake enough	Bake more bread!

PRACTICE AND VARIATIONS

I recommend that you practice this chapter's recipe a few more times before you move on to the next part of the book. Even if this one turned out great, which I hope it did, repeating it a few times will give you more experience and more opportunities to get a feel for what works when you're applying heat to your dough!

If you want some variety, here are some suggestions:

A SWEETER BREAD

Add 2–3 tablespoons of sugar or ⅛ cup of honey to the ingredients. Be aware that additional sugar will give more for the yeast to chomp on and the bread will rise a little faster.

GARLIC AND HERBS

Mince up 2–3 cloves of garlic. Add them to the mix, along with some of your favorite herbs, like rosemary, basil, or parsley.

CHEESE BREAD

Add a handful of grated cheddar or jack cheese to the mix. Stir it up well, and it will melt in as it bakes, infusing a wonderful tang to the whole loaf. Some of the cheese bits might stick to the bottom of the Dutch oven, making the bread difficult to remove when it's done. It might be a good idea to put a circle of parchment paper on the bottom of the Dutch oven while it's preheating so the loaf will still drop right out when it's done.

TOPPINGS

In those few moments that you have after you drop in the dough and before you close it up in the heat, you can put some things on top. Sprinkle on some sesame seeds, kosher salt, or brown sugar. Brush on a beaten egg, for shine, or spread on some butter for a richer taste. Remember that you want to close up the lid as fast as possible, so have it all ready by your side before you open the preheated Dutch oven.

Rubbing a butter stick over the loaf as soon as it's on the cooling rack also adds flavor and richness and will soften the top crust.

Try all of these and see which ones you like! Each time you do, remember to feel the heat and learn what it feels like. Also, savor the taste and smells, learning what each one is like. Analyze the crust and the crumb, and check the troubleshooting table.

Chapter 2
A Simple Kneaded Bread

I HOPE you've had your first taste (pun maliciously intended) of success with the no-knead bread. It's easy to see why it has become such a hit with the home-baking crowd. It's easy, simple, and delicious. The long rise time not only gives it the time to develop the gluten that's so important for the structure of the bread, but it also helps give the dough the richer, deeper flavors.

Next, however, I'd like to bring you to the vast world of the kneaded breads. This one is also geared to help you get some quick success—it's a tasty recipe, and it's not too difficult to pull off. By far, traditional breads are kneaded more often than not, so it's important to learn how to do it.

Between the no-knead bread and this one, I'm honestly not sure which one I like better. They're both great but different. Sometimes I want to make bread all in one afternoon. I can't do the overnight or even the six-hour rise that a no-knead would require.

I also think that the crumb structure is generally more developed in a kneaded bread. A kneaded loaf generally has a tight, smooth surface, which will bake into a rich, brown, caramelized crust. Yum!

Okay, I guess I do generally like the kneaded breads a little bit better. . . . But not exclusively!

Jodi's Family's Sweet Sandwich Bread

Before we dive in and start working the dough in our fingers, let me talk a little about this recipe and why I chose it for the first kneaded bread. It came from my mother-in-law. My wife, Jodi, has made it for us in the kitchen many times over the years. It has a rich and sweet flavor, which I really like. Even though it's sweet, I like it with savory meats and tangy condiments. Sweet toppings work too. A PB&J with this bread rocks!

The flavor comes mainly from the enrichments: egg, oil, and honey. The recipe in the previous chapter was fairly bare, with just flour, water, yeast, and salt. I wanted to keep it simple and easy to do, with fewer ingredients. Learning to make bread with a plain recipe is important—you can discover the wonderful and complex flavors that come from the flour and the yeast themselves, rather than all of the enrichments.

Oddly enough, with a kneaded bread, I had a harder time with only the bare four ingredients. I was much more successful when I had the enrichments to help out. The honey helped the flavor and gave the yeast more energy in the rise. The oil gave richness to the flavor. The milk added fluff to the crumb structure, helped out by the egg.

Making a light and stretchy loaf of this bread without all those enhancements was an exciting challenge. We can leave that for more advanced efforts. For your first loaf of kneaded bread, let's use all the help we can!

MORE BASIC TOOLS

You'll need pretty much everything listed in the previous chapter (page 13) to do the process in this chapter as well. Here are some other things you'll also need:

Small mixing bowl or cup: This should be large enough to hold a couple cups of liquid. You'll be using it to wake up the yeast. You'll also want it to not be a reactive metal. Plastic is best.

Flour sifter: Not absolutely necessary, but I prefer to use it.

1 tablespoon measuring spoon

Bread dough cutter: This is a small square of metal with one straight edge and some kind of grip on the opposite edge. It's used to chop the dough into chunks. It's not absolutely necessary; you can use your hands, but I like using the cutter.

2–3 clean, dry tea towels

Razor blade: Use a razor blade to cut scores in the top of the loaf so it can vent steam and expand better. This could even be a hobby knife. Make sure that it's very sharp; I've found that even my chef's knife is not sharp enough. You need it razor-blade sharp. If it's not, it will tear the dough instead of slicing through it.

INGREDIENTS

1 cup hot water: The ideal temperature to activate the yeast is 110–115 degrees Fahrenheit. I tested that once, and in my mind, that's about the temperature of a hot shower. In this case, since you'll be adding in honey, I'd make it really, really hot. The honey will cool it back down, hopefully to something close to that temperature.

Some tap waters have chlorine in them, which, as I mentioned previously, can inhibit the yeast growth. Filtered or bottled water is good. However, I've made good bread with tap water too, so . . . ya know . . . use what ya got.

¾ cup honey

1 Tbsp. yeast: Ordinary baker's yeast from the grocery store. It doesn't need to be instant yeast or fresh cake baker's yeast. Let's keep this simple!

4–5 cups flour, plus more for kneading: This needs to be bread flour and relatively fresh as well. Why bread flour? Why not all-purpose (AP) flour? Why not self-rising flour? Why not whole-wheat flour?

Okay, one question at a time. First of all, let me tell you why the flour should be fresh. Early in my experience, I got a 25-pound bag of flour, excited that it would last me for a long time. After only a few months, I had a difficult time kneading to the point where I would get good gluten. First, the flour was getting old, and second, I wasn't storing it right. I learned a lesson, and will never go back. I get smaller bags of bread flour, I store it in airtight containers, and I use it up and replenish it.

There is a difference between bread flours and AP flours. Flours designed and milled for bread have higher protein levels, so they develop gluten more easily.

Self-rising flour is AP flour wherein baking powder and sodas have been added. Obviously, you don't want that for yeast breads, and frankly, I'd rather be able to control the proportions of the chemical leavens when I make biscuits and soda breads anyway. So I never use self-rising flour.

Whole-wheat flour is great, but this isn't a whole-wheat recipe, so. . . .

A pinch of salt: Actually, I'd go with a big pinch, or a couple small ones.

1 cup milk: I usually use fresh milk from a jug. I'd heard that it has enzymes that can inhibit yeast growth. It turns out that pasteurization breaks down those enzymes. If you mix the milk from a powder, it also won't have them. It's also not a bad idea to leave the milk out to warm to ambient temperature. That will help with the yeast growth later on as well. Also, we usually drink 2 percent milk at our house, so that's what I use. Richer milks will yield richer breads.

1 egg: Leaving it out a while to come up to room temperature is cool too.

2 Tbsp. oil: Veggie oil, olive oil . . . use what you like. I like olive oil.

"CHEATER" INGREDIENTS

I do want to say a word or two about a couple of ingredients that are becoming more popular in the bread-baking world: vital wheat gluten and dough enhancer.

Vital wheat gluten is a powder of the protein that has been extracted from the wheat berry. It's what forms the gluten strands that trap the gas and give the bread its structure. There are some cases where it will be important to add it. Some folks like to put it in ordinary white bread, but if you're already using bread flour, and it's fresh, you shouldn't need it.

Dough enhancer is purported to give a better crumb structure and a better rise. When you read the ingredients on the side, you'll see why. It adds extra yeast, soy lecithin or egg solids, vital wheat gluten, and even vitamin C. All of these things do just what they say it will do. But, if you're following a good recipe, most of that will be in there anyway. Well, except for vitamin C, but that's easy enough to add—simply grind in a vitamin C tablet.

My point is that these things are not necessary, and I would recommend not using them so you don't rely on them as a crutch.

I will admit that I use them, particularly the vital wheat gluten, when I'm using flour that I know is old, or if I have to use or supplement the flour with AP flour. But by and large, I don't need these additives.

MIXING

Put the hot water in the small mixing bowl or cup. Again, it can be really hot, but not boiling. Add the honey to it and stir it up. If you want, you can watch the temperature and adjust it up or down, by heating it up or letting it cool, to the 110–115 range. I've found that after adding the honey, the temperature will be close, generally on the cool side.

Add the yeast and stir it up. Let it sit for 10–15 minutes. This is often called "proofing" or "proving" the yeast. I don't call it that myself, because other steps in the breadmaking process are also referred to as "proofing," and I get confused really easily! I like to think of this step as "waking" the yeast. Others call it "activating" the yeast.

Ideally, after the wait, you should see some foam gathering at the top of the water. This is the yeast multiplying and belching out the CO_2 that will eventually make the bread rise. Give it a sniff. It will have a familiar yeasty, bready smell that you'll come to love.

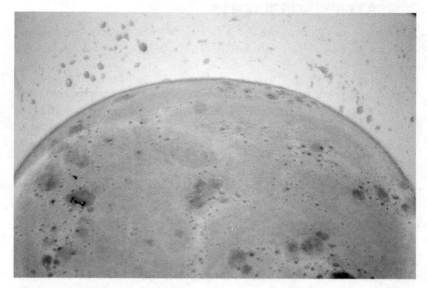

If you don't see a lot of foam, that's okay. The yeast is still probably alive and well. It could simply be that the water was cooled too much by the honey so it didn't grow and activate quite as quickly.

Now scoop up the flour and sift it into the large mixing bowl. When you scoop, don't pack the flour into the measuring cup. Let it be loose. I dip the measuring cup in and then shake it side-to-side to level it off. You can use the method where you dip and scrape it level with a knife if you want. You don't *need* to sift the flour, but I almost always do. It does break up chunks, which isn't really a big problem, but the real reason is to aerate the flour. This will make it a bit more fluffy. Sprinkle on the salt.

Then add the yeast mixture to the large mixing bowl, followed by all the other ingredients. It's easiest to simply make a big well in the middle of the flour and pour everything into it, one by one.

Then grab your wooden spoon and start mixing: I start slowly, like I'm folding the ingredients together. I cut from the middle of the bowl to the edge, then turn the bowl and do it again. Soon it will all be a bit more blended and I can start stirring. It will be stiff and probably still sticky. I like to start the dough with too little flour because I'll add it constantly as I'm kneading.

Once it's all fairly blended together, it's time to start kneading.

KNEADING

Kneading serves a lot of purposes. First of all, and most important, it develops the gluten strands out of the protein in the flour. When you have higher protein flour—like bread flour—and water, over time you'll get gluten. The strands of gluten give the bread that stretchy feel, give the crumb structure, and, especially, trap the CO_2 gas that the yeast germs are belching out. That makes the bread rise, filled with bubbles. When it bakes, the heat first expands the gases and makes the bread swell immediately and then sets the crumb in place, leaving that chewy and stretchy texture.

In the last recipe, you let the gluten develop over time with the overnight rise. In this recipe, you're going to help it along with agitation.

Another thing that kneading does is to thoroughly mix the ingredients throughout the mass. This will make the yeast come in contact with more flour and sugar, which it needs to eat to make the gases. It will also come in contact with the salt, which tempers or slows the yeast growth. We do that just to keep it under control. Without the salt, the yeast would go nuts and the bread would rise too fast. Plus, the salt helps bring out the flavor of the flour.

Finally, the kneading helps to adjust to the perfect amount of flour. Different flours on different days will absorb more or less water. I like to start by mixing in less flour and adding it to the dough in the kneading process. That way, I can "creep up" to just the right amount to get just the right texture.

I like to knead by hand. I've really got nothing against a mixer, but, as I've said before, most Dutch oven cook-offs don't allow them, and I actually like the feel of the dough in my hands. I use that feel to tell how much flour to add. I also use it to know when the kneading is done. There is, however, a specific test that I'll mention in a minute.

Sprinkle a generous amount of flour onto the workspace that you have, be it a kitchen counter, a camping table, or whatever ya gots! Scoop the dough out of the bowl onto the flour. The dough that you've mixed in the steps so far should actually be pretty loose and sticky. I like to scrape as much of the goo out of the bowl as possible. Sprinkle more flour over the top and begin working it in your hands.

I'm not aware of any one "best" way to knead. I usually start out with one hand, smooshing the dough between my fingers, picking it up, and dropping it back in a different place and position. Then I grab it again and keep doing the same thing. I also press in with the heel of my palm and then fold it over and do it again. Sometimes I'll do two heels at once.

At first, since the dough will be sticky, it will get all over your hands. Sprinkle on more flour as you go. As soon as you add the flour, it will stick less, but then as the flour gets blended in and absorbed, it gets sticky again.

I use the bread cutter to scrape the dough up off the table, and I'll frequently add more flour to the tabletop as well. I often will add as much as a cup or two of flour over time.

When it starts to clean the dough off of my hands and fingers and not leave more sticky dough behind, the dough is getting to the point where the flour/water balance is good.

If you use this process, you'll probably get the balance correct. Sometimes, however, I have added too much flour, and it needs to be wet. It's not as easy to put liquid back into the dough. One way is to spritz water on my hands and knead it back in.

If I'm using fresh bread flour, this will usually be about the point when the gluten is getting well developed also. I don't time my kneading. Again, different flours react differently on different days. Simply to say, "Knead for 10 minutes" is not going to tell me if it's ready or not. By the same token, "Knead until it's silky smooth" is pretty meaningless as well, unless you've already been baking bread for years.

That's why I love the "Windowpane Test." This is a way of determining if the gluten has developed enough, and if the dough is ready. First, cut off or pinch off a small chunk of the dough (see photo on next page).

Then roll it into a ball.

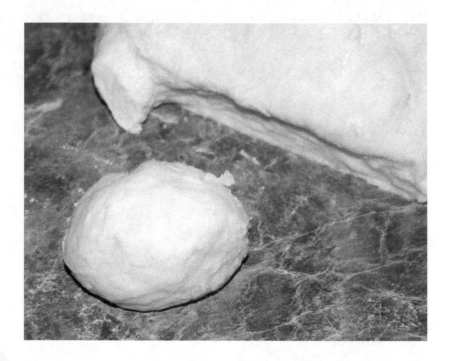

Flatten that ball and begin to work it and stretch it, like a tiny pizza dough. As you stretch it thinner and thinner, notice when it finally tears. If you can get it to be a translucent "windowpane" without tearing, you'll know that the dough is ready.

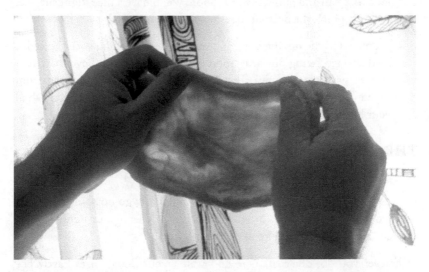

As you get more and more used to the kneading process, you'll also notice that the surface of the kneaded doughball becomes more smooth and stretchy and doesn't tear as much as you're nearing the end of kneading. It will feel different in your hands as you near readiness. I can't describe that in any definitive way, however. It does feel smooth, even "satiny," but what does that mean? You'll get it eventually. In the meantime, the test works. Actually, I still use the test.

Sometimes, with good flour and good kneading, it might only take 10 minutes or so to get a successful "windowpane." Sometimes, it's much longer. There have been times that, after 35 minutes of mushing and pounding, I've finally given up. The bread still rises, but not as high or as quickly, and it's not the same texture in the end. When that happens, it's usually because the flour is older or doesn't have as much protein to make into gluten.

Once you've gotten a good windowpane and you can tell that the bread is well kneaded, form it into a ball. One way to do this is to "pull and tuck." Pull the top surface of the bread tight by stretching it out to the sides. Then tuck what you pulled under the bottom. Turn the ball in your hands and do it again. This will leave a nice tight gluten surface on the bread. Pinch the bottom, where everything was tucked, together tightly.

Another way, which is trickier but more fun to do, is to set the dough on your tabletop (there shouldn't be any flour left on it at this point) and cup both hands over it. With a very light touch, but keeping your hands on the dough, move the doughball around in a circle. The tabletop will grip the bottom of the ball and pull it inward. Soon, you'll have a nice, tight surface. Then, simply pinch the bottom together and you're ready!

Spray some oil in the mixing bowl and put the doughball in, with the tight, stretched surface facing upward. Spray it with oil as well. Cover it with a tea towel or with plastic wrap. The oil and the covering will keep it from drying out during the rising period. Otherwise, you'll have a crackly shell over your bread, and it won't bake right.

THE FIRST RISE

This is both the easiest and the hardest part of the preparation for me.

It's easy because you don't do anything. You simply go do something else for a couple of hours. Read a book. Watch TV. Clean your house. Go to church. Do whatever you like to do.

Whatever you do, don't sit there and watch your dough rise. Partly because that would be incredibly boring but mostly because it would be much harder to tell when the dough is risen.

It's hard because watching for the bread to rise is always nerve wracking. If I've used good bread flour, I've kneaded enough, I've done everything right, and I've bowed to the right baking gods that morning, then the dough will rise just fine. If not, I'll have a dead hunk of flour that, if baked, will turn into a brick.

The best environment for dough to rise is about 80 degrees. That's a bit warmer than I feel comfortable in, so I don't recommend cranking up the furnace or turning off the air conditioner. I've found that bread will rise quite nicely at a tasty room temperature of 72 degrees. If you want, you can create a bread-rising environment by turning on an indoor oven to the lowest setting and watching the heat with an oven thermometer. Remember that yeast will start dying if it gets higher than 120 degrees, and it will die completely at 140. When the oven is warm, keep the door open and keep monitoring the temperature. Put the dough in and wait.

I've also heard of people starting their dishwasher with hot water, turning it off, and using the warm, wet space to raise the dough. I haven't tried this one myself.

If you're out in the wild and it's chilly out, you can put some coals on a Dutch oven and use it as a rising space. I would start with 4 coals above. Coals placed below the Dutch oven can get the oven too hot. After about 15 minutes, check the interior temperature with an oven thermometer. If it's still cool, add more coals until you get the right temperature. Then maintain that many coals to keep the temperature the same during the rise time.

Count on at least one hour as rise time, but possibly as much as two to two and a half hours. So many factors can impact the time of a rise: the temperature, the quality and age of the flour, the quality and amount of the yeast, how much gluten is formed in the kneading, and so on.

Most recipes say to let it rise until it's "doubled in bulk." Frankly, that's tough to estimate. On the other hand, every other method I've ever heard of (like poking the dough with your finger) is about as useful and accurate. So I just eyeball it and guess when it's about twice as big. In some cases, it will also be influenced by how much time I have available as well. There have been many times when I've ended a rise because I needed to get the process movin' on, even though I didn't really think it was fully ready. If I'm not under a deadline, or if that deadline isn't as pressing, I like to err on the long side, rather than the short side.

Here's an interesting twist: What if you *want* a long rise? What if, for flavor's sake, or because of intervening events, you want it to take longer to rise?

Well, if you can speed it up by raising the temperature a bit, you can also slow it by cooling it down! There have been times when I have mixed and kneaded my dough before church, and, knowing that I wouldn't be back in time to catch the end of the rise, I put it in the fridge (covered, of course). It would still rise a bit, but not so much. Then, when I returned, I pulled it out and let it warm up a bit before the next step. It's a good idea to let it rise for a bit, sort of to get started, before putting it in the fridge. Once it's in the fridge, you can leave it in there for quite some time, even overnight. The end result, after you pull it out and warm it up, needs to still be about doubled in bulk.

Once the initial rise is done, it's time for the next step!

PREP FOR BAKING: COALS, SHAPING, PROOFING, PREHEATING

As soon as I decide that the dough is ready, even before I start working with it again, I go out to my Dutch oven cooking area and light up some coals. I'll want 35–40 coals. It'll take a while for them to burn and get white edges, and it'll take more time for them to preheat the Dutch oven. In the meantime, I'll prepare the dough for baking.

SHAPING

You can shape bread many different ways. There are a lot of traditional shapes, and many of those are associated with particular recipes and procedures. French bread, for example, is usually a long torpedo shape. Most "artisan" breads are a simple ball loaf. Challah is usually braided. You can make dozens of different shapes of rolls.

For this loaf, we're going to make a simple artisan *boule* (that's French for "ball").

Lightly dust the tabletop with flour. When I say "lightly," I mean "very lightly." You really won't need much to keep it from sticking, and too much can actually make creating the shapes you're shooting for more difficult. Drop or peel the doughball out onto your tabletop. Right away, it will lose some size and shape as the gas bubbles break. That's okay—it will rise again. Drape a tea towel or some other dry, clean cloth in the mixing/rising bowl. Sprinkle some flour over its now-concave surface. You're ready to go.

Roll the dough around a little. You're not kneading it, but you do want to work it a bit. One thing this process does is to redistribute the yeast and the flour inside a little so there's some fresh yeast growth. Still, you don't want to press out *all* of the gas!

Then, re-create the doughball like you had before. Pull and tuck like you probably did earlier to create a tight surface. This will make for a smooth browned crust. If you hadn't degassed it completely, it should be a little bit bigger than your first doughball, before the first rise. Set it on the cloth in the bowl, with the stretched side down and the crimped side up. Make sure that it's well crimped or it will open up as it continues to rise.

Why set it on the cloth? Why place it "face down"? Because these things will make the dough easier to handle when the baking time comes.

By this point, the coals might be hot. If not, give them a few more minutes.

Spray or wipe some oil around the inside of a 12-inch shallow Dutch oven and take it to the coals, with the lid on. Set 10–12 coals in a ring around the bottom edge, and 22–24 in a ring on the lid. In bread baking, I tend to err toward more coals rather than less. In 15–20 minutes, the Dutch oven will be nicely preheated, and you're ready to bake! Leave the extra coals aside.

In the meantime, gather your razor blade and your thermometer and keep them handy.

BAKING

After 15–20 minutes of preheating, the Dutch oven should be ready and the doughball will have re-risen. It won't double in bulk again, but it should be somewhere in between that and where it was. The steps that follow should be done quickly so as to minimize the loss of heat and to minimize handling of the dough. Gather the dough and the razor near the cooking space.

Then, lift the lid and set it aside. Turn the dough into the Dutch oven. It might sizzle a bit when it hits the hot oven bottom. The cloth will keep it from sticking to the bowl and will allow you to manipulate the dough more easily. Whisk the cloth away. You should be looking at the smooth stretched surface of the dough. Quickly take your razor and slash it. I usually do three quick parallel slashes, about a half inch deep. You can do a cross, if you want, or even a spiral. It doesn't matter. The slashes allow the dough to spring, or expand, without tearing the crust, and they also allow steam to vent.

The venting steam, by the way, will be trapped under the heavy Dutch oven lid and will help to develop a richer, crunchier crust!

Quickly cover the Dutch oven again and mark the time.

Oh, and toss 6–8 fresh coals on your "aside" pile so you have a few extras if you need them. You might not, but it's best to have them and not ruin your bread.

Now relax for a while. Not too long, but you can kick back with a soda and a magazine. Or call a friend. Just don't lose track of the time.

After about 15 minutes, rotate the Dutch oven. Using the lid lifter, lift the entire Dutch oven and rotate it about a quarter turn. Then rotate the lid about a quarter turn. Once you've done this, the relative positions of the coals, the Dutch oven, and the bread ball will be different. That way, hot spots are less likely to develop on the bottom, and if they do develop on the lid, they'll have less impact on the baking.

Also, take your thermometer, lift the lid, and stick the probe down into the bread. Make sure that the dial is in a readable position and close the lid very quickly. In the process, you'll probably also get a good look at how the crust is starting to form and brown. The loaf should have gotten significantly bigger too. This is referred to as "spring" and is the result of all of that gas trapped in the gluten strands being suddenly heated and expanding by exposure to the hot air of the Dutch oven.

Tap away the ashes on the coals, bottom and top. Too much ash on the coals will actually insulate them, and they'll radiate less heat. Finally, take a look at the coals themselves. If they're burned down pretty small, then add 3 or so to the bottom and the top, evenly spaced. Maybe more on the top. I usually don't add more. They would have to be really burned down for me to do that. The natural burning cycle of the coals that I use gives a nice, gradual lowering of the temperature, and the bread is usually done long before they burn out. Still, wind, cold weather, and other conditions can change that, so keep an eye on the coals.

Go back to relaxing for a bit longer. This would also be a good time to make sure that you have a cooling rack set up and hot pads or oven gloves handy.

After another 15–20 minutes, lift the lid and quickly check the thermometer. All of the traditional tests for doneness (golden-brown crust, thumping the bottom) don't really work in the world of Dutch ovens. A thermometer will tell me if it's done or doughy. It should read between 190 and 200 degrees. If it doesn't, put the lid back on, rotate the oven again, and leave it on the coals for another 5–10 minutes, depending on how close the temperature is.

If it is done, set the lid aside and bring the Dutch oven to the cooling rack. Using the gloves or the hot pads, turn the bread out and quickly turn it over to cool right side up on the cooling rack. While you're turning it over, take a look at the bottom crust. Is it brown but not burned? Are there any spots of uneven color?

Congratulations! If all went well, you've just had your first successful loaf of kneaded bread.

COOLING

. . . But actually, it's not done cooking yet. That's why you should resist the urge to cut into it right away. Inside, the bread is still cooking. The structures are still solidifying, and the flavors are still changing. Let it sit and relax. You do the same! Let it cool fully. I know hot bread is wonderful, but trust me, it will be better if you wait.

If you want to, you can spread some butter across the upper crust to melt into it and soften it while you wait. It will naturally soften some on its own while it cools, while the heated moisture from inside the crumb migrates outward.

I used to let the bread cool in the Dutch oven. I later learned that the same moisture that softens the upper crust as it escapes to the air will make the bottom crust soggy, since there is no place to escape to. That can be tricky if you're baking rolls and you want to be able to remove them intact, in one piece, for presentation's sake in a cook-off, for example. In that case, it would be wise to place some parchment paper strips across the bottom of the Dutch oven, draped over the edge, before baking. They can be used to lift the rolls out, as a single complete mass, and onto the cooling rack.

Protect the bread from thieves and enemies within during this most delicate part of the process. In my house, we have two dogs, and if I'm not vigilant, they'll grab my loaves and run. It's often difficult to keep the kids away from it as well when the rich yeasty aroma advertises the arrival of home-baked goodness. Fight for your bread!

EATING

Finally, you get to eat it!

For this bread, I usually slice it across the middle and then slice that half in half, making a quarter-loaf wedge. With this, I'll make individual slices for butter, honey, jam, or sandwiches. Be sure to taste some of it straight, without any toppings, so you can learn what it's supposed to taste like. Judge each attempt to measure your progress.

POSSIBLE PROBLEMS

Here are some bits of advice for troubleshooting possible problems. This will be similar to the table in the previous chapter, with a few variations.

Problem	What's Probably Wrong	What to Try Next Time
Doesn't rise as much	Not enough gluten, or yeast not very active	This is most likely because of inadequate kneading. If you didn't use the windowpane test or if you didn't knead long enough—in either case, there wouldn't have been enough gluten strands to trap the gas the yeast was belching out. If you kneaded a lot but still couldn't get a good windowpane, the flour might have been old. Try again with fresher flour or add some vital wheat gluten to your next batch.

Problem	What's Probably Wrong	What to Try Next Time
Doughy inside	Not done	Make sure that the tip of the thermometer sensor lead is in the center of the bread loaf so it can measure the temperature accurately. For that matter, make sure your thermometer is accurate. Keeping a good balance between bottom and top heat steadily throughout the cooking process can make a big difference. Also, make sure the bread cools completely before eating.
Hard or burned bottom crust	Too much bottom heat, especially in the later stages of baking	Getting the proper balance between top and bottom heat comes with practice. When you replenish the bottom coals, don't put as many on, or wait longer to replenish.
Burned top crust	Too much top heat, especially in the later stages of baking	When you replenish the top coals, don't put as many on, or wait longer to replenish. Also, don't leave top heat on as long if you do extended cooking at the end.
Not much "spring"	Oven not preheated enough	Put more coals on or wait longer for the preheat.
Heavy and dense, not light and fluffy	Not risen enough, or not enough heat	If the bread doesn't rise enough, it might not be getting enough gases trapped in the dough, so it doesn't expand in the oven. Also, if the oven isn't preheated or hot enough overall, then the gas that is trapped won't expand as much. Make sure that the dough is well risen and that the oven is good and hot.

Problem	What's Probably Wrong	What to Try Next Time
Spots that are more brown than others	Uneven heat	Make sure that the coals are spaced in a ring fairly evenly both underneath the oven and on the lid above. Remember to turn the lid and Dutch oven every 10–15 minutes to prevent hot spots.
Bread is gone too quickly	You did a great job but didn't bake enough	Bake more bread!

Now that you've taken the time to learn the basic no-knead bread and a simple kneaded bread, and now that you've had some taste of success, let's take some time in the next chapter to really learn about what's going on in a great loaf. We'll talk about the ingredients and the details of the processes. Then, in the following chapters, I'll share more recipes!

Let's go!

Chapter 3
The Breadmaking Process

MANY DIFFERENT kinds of yeast breads exist. Some have unique ingredients. Others will be made using different steps and processes. Some use the same recipes and processes but are simply shaped differently.

Even with all the variation, they all have underlying similarities. If you understand the big picture of the process, you'll be able to use that process to make a better loaf of whatever kind it is that you're trying to make.

Really, that's what we're trying to do here. We're trying to control ingredients and processes to bring about a better final result. This is the 2 percent!

STEP 1: PREPARATION, PLANNING, INGREDIENTS

"MISE EN PLACE"

This concept is taught in culinary school and used in running restaurants. It's pronounced "meez ahn plas," and it means "putting in place." The idea is to have everything (ingredients, tools, space) ready when you start so you don't have to dig and search for anything in a hurry right when you need it.

Honestly, I don't always do this. I'm not that well-organized. Yet, when I do follow mise en place, the cooking experience always goes smoother, with better results, and I end up less frustrated.

You'd think I'd learn my lesson, eh?

In breadmaking, however, there are several stages. Some breads take as much as three days to make. In those cases, I'll set up my mise en place as I approach each stage of the process.

Here, for your reference, are the basic tools for Dutch oven breadmaking. For detailed thoughts on these, refer back to chapters one and two (if you've been cooking along with the book, you'll already have these):

   large plastic or ceramic mixing bowl

   small plastic or ceramic mixing bowl or cup

   wooden spoon

   1 cup measuring cup

   1 teaspoon measuring spoon

   1 tablespoon measuring spoon

   flour sifter (optional)

   countertop or flat working surface

   extra flour

   spray oil

   2–3 clean, dry tea towels

   bread dough cutter (optional)

   proofing baskets (optional)

razor blade

12-inch shallow Dutch oven

40 or more charcoal briquettes

matches, lighter fluid, or some other way of igniting the coals

Dutch oven lid lifter

coal tongs

cooking surface for the Dutch oven

leave-in thermometer that will measure up to 200 degrees

gloves or hot pads

cooling rack

Mise en place is also a bit of mental preparation. Which leads me to . . .

PLANNING

The first thing to do, really, is to read over the recipe and plan your time. The stages of breadmaking require both times of great flurried activity (like mixing, kneading, shaping) and times of patient waiting (like rising, baking). Look ahead at the time you have to make the bread and see if any interruptions are likely to arise. Plan to have those interruptions happen in the downtimes of the steps, if possible.

For example, I do much of my cooking on Sundays. So, I've worked out a great plan where I will often mix my dough in the morning before going to the neighborhood church, and then when I come home, it's nicely risen (assuming the dogs didn't get to the dough).

When I do one of my drawn-out sourdoughs, I plan out when, each night, I can prepare the starter, the barm, and finally the bread.

The point is to know in advance how it's likely to play out so you can still run your life. As much as I'd like to think that there's nothing more to life than a good loaf of bread, that's just not reality!

INGREDIENTS

The core ingredients of bread are:

flour

yeast

salt

water

One thing I learned the hard way is that ingredients matter. Using low-quality stuff, or even high-quality stuff that's old, will impact your results, even to the point of failure. That's especially true of the flour.

FLOUR

WHITE BREAD FLOUR

Most of the recipes in this book are variations on some sort of white bread. Even though I grew up eating almost nothing but whole-wheat bread, and even though these days everyone is talking about how bad white bread is for you and how wonderful whole grains are, I still love the flavor. I also love how variable, how adaptable it is. If eating it is wrong, then I don't wanna be right. Maybe moderation is the key, okay?

I am getting more and more picky about the flours I use. Not so much picky about the brands but definitely the types. When baking yeast breads, I only use bread flour. My wife used to razz me about that and call me a "food snob." But bread flour has more of the proteins that form gluten. Bread flour is 12–14 percent protein. As you knead, that protein will develop into gluten and produce a smoother texture. It will also make it easier to stretch and shape the dough and will give it a soft, smooth, elastic surface tension. When it rises, the gluten strands will trap the gas better and the dough will rise more. When it bakes, you will get that soft, chewy crumb and the rich browned crust.

Storing bread flour correctly is also important. Once you've opened the bag, keep it airtight. Exposure to air will speed the oxidization of the fatty acids from the wheat germ. Keeping the flour completely free of air is impossible, so plan on using the flour as quickly as possible. Bread flour has a shelf life of 4–6 months tops. However, I notice that kneading becomes harder after only 2½–3 months of bread flour's shelf life. I used to buy big bags of flour. Now I buy smaller quantities and buy it more often. Fresh is the key!

I've learned these things by hard experience. Using old flour or non–bread flour will keep the dough from rising as much beforehand and springing in the oven, and you could end up with a baked brick, suitable for little more than a doorstop. Trust me. I've been there. It's not pretty!

ALL-PURPOSE FLOUR

All-purpose flour typically has a protein content of 10–12 percent. It's a compromise flour; it's not cake flour, but it's not really bread flour either. Some say that you can use it for bread. In a pinch, where there's nothing else, I'd do it, but I go into the process knowing that I'll have to knead it a *lot* more. Sometimes, if I have to use AP flour, I'll add in a tablespoon or two of vital wheat gluten powder. That can sometimes make up the difference, and the dough will be workable.

Since I don't use AP flour for yeast bread and I don't use it for cakes, what's it good for, then?

Lots! I use it for any kind of cooking or baking where gluten formation isn't critical: pancakes, biscuits, soda breads, cookies, fruit breads (like banana bread), tortillas, roux, papier-mâché glue, and many others. All of those recipes that use chemical leavens like baking soda or baking powder work great with AP flour.

Even though I still try to keep AP flour airtight and as fresh as possible, I've found that its storage isn't as critical as bread flour's.

CAKE FLOUR

Of the white flours, cake flour has the lowest protein content, at about 6–9 percent. It's also more finely milled, so it yields a light and fluffy cake. In yeast breads, cake flour is totally unusable.

SELF-RISING FLOUR

Bleh. No thanks! I won't touch self-rising flour. This is basically an all-purpose flour that already has baking powder mixed in. I guess it's supposed to be a convenience for you. Obviously, for a yeast bread, you wouldn't want the chemical reactions going on, messing up the yeast growth. And, when I'm making a soda bread or biscuits, I like to be able to control the proportion of chemical leaven to flour rather than relying on what the miller decided.

WHOLE-WHEAT FLOUR

You can find many kinds and brands of whole-wheat flours. They are, as the name implies, the whole grain, ground into flour. The bran and the germ are not extracted. This makes it much healthier to eat, with more fiber and nutrients. Whole-wheat bread also has a much denser loaf, so it takes some getting used to if you're more accustomed to light, fluffy white breads.

Whole wheat is particularly useful for food storage. You simply store a plastic five-gallon tub of wheat grain, and when you want to bake, run it through a grinder (electric or hand) and you have flour. I've used both hand grinders and electric ones, and I'm telling you, I prefer the electric ones! Not only can they ground finer and more consistent flour, but the hand grinders can be a real workout!

Still, if you're trying to feed your family while your spouse is taking a turn defending the homestead from the onslaught of the zombic apocalypse and the power utilities have long since shut down, a hand-cranked wheat mill would do just fine.

Whole-wheat flour, even though its protein levels are at about 13 percent, does not produce much gluten on its own. As a result, many "whole-wheat" breads are actually made from a mixture of whole-wheat flour and white flour. This helps to produce a whole wheat loaf with a lighter crumb, so more people who like white bread are apt to buy it.

You can also add in vital wheat gluten powder to increase the gluten-ity of the flour.

OTHER GRAINS AND FLOURS

Just about every grain known to man can be ground up and made into a flour. Rye, barley, corn, and oats are some of the more common non-wheat flours. They all have different flavors, textures, and, of course, protein levels. Most of them will require some kind of help in the gluten department if you're making a yeast-risen bread. Personally, a good rye bread is one of my favorite flavors in baking. I just can't get enough of that!

FLOUR ADDITIVES

As I mentioned before, if you're using an old bread flour, an all-purpose flour, or a whole-wheat flour, you'll probably want to add some vital wheat gluten to the mix. This is a powdered version of flour with everything but the proteins removed—almost. It's usually about 75 percent protein. Typically, you'll use a tablespoon or so for every 2–3 cups of flour. It will also absorb more liquid, so be aware of that as you're mixing/kneading.

Dough enhancer is a bread dough additive that I've been seeing more and more in recent years. It contains a lot of ingredients designed to improve the overall texture and rise of bread. The ingredients is a big list of things that help.

It adds things like extra yeast and vitamin C, which spurs yeast growth, for more rise. It has gluten powder, to help get that chewiness and to better trap the yeast gas. Soy lecithin is an agent to help the crumb structure solidify, much like egg white does. Do you need dough enhancer? Not really. You can learn to make great bread without it. But it doesn't hurt either.

YEAST

What kind of yeast should you buy and use?

Active dry yeast is the most common supermarket yeast. I usually use this. I get a big block of it and store it in the freezer, where it will keep for up to a year. You have to "proof," or "activate," it before you use it, usually in water at about 110 degrees. It rises faster than a wild-caught sourdough yeast but slower than a rapid-rise commercial yeast. Remember, a fast rise isn't always the most flavorful rise.

Instant yeast has a little more yeast bugs packed into smaller granules, so you need less, and the medium in which the yeast germs are suspended dissolves more quickly, so you don't have to "proof" it. You can simply add it into the flour and other dry ingredients, and it will dissolve and activate when you mix in the wet ingredients. It doesn't have as long of a shelf-life, however.

Rapid-rise yeast is best suited for breadmaking machines. It packs a lot of germ *oomph* into small granules, so the multiplication and activation happens quickly. You might not always want a short rise, though. You might want to take some time and develop more flavor. On the other hand, if you're doing a cook-off and you're in a time crunch, this could help!

Wild-caught yeasts are a lot of fun to work with and have a rich flavor all of their own, but they take much more fuss and time. To catch the bugs in the first place, you have to take as long as a week of working up a starter, then it has to be carefully preserved, cared for, and fed in your fridge to be able to keep. This yeast tends to rise a little more slowly than commercial yeasts. Again, this is not always a bad thing.

Other kinds of yeasts exist: cream, cake, brick. But these are usually more for commercial bakeries, and they are hard to get and store for a home or back-porch chef.

SALT

There really isn't much to say about salt. It's, you know . . . salt. It's there to regulate the yeast growth. It's there for extra flavor, because salt, like a good brother, brings out the better flavors in everything else.

These days, you can find many different kinds of designer salts: sea salt, flavored salt, Himalayan salt, kosher salt. . . . Which to use? It doesn't really matter much. Try them all.

One caveat: if you try a coarse grain variety, use more. Since the grains are larger, there are bigger gaps between the grains as you pour them into a measuring spoon. As a result, less actual salt gets in. Smaller grains, more salt.

WATER

Not really much to say about water, either. Except this: some tap waters contain heavier doses of chlorine, which can inhibit or kill off your yeasts. Lately, since I have easy access to it, I've been using filtered water, with good results. Honestly, I've often used my own tap water, and the yeast has been fine. Your mileage may vary.

Oh, this too: Many of the recipes will suggest or require that the temperature of the water be at about 110 degrees. I adjusted my tap water once under a thermometer to see what 110 degrees felt like. To me, it's just a little bit hotter than I like my showers. Knowing that makes it easy to quickly get the water to a good temperature. I would recommend you do the same experiment and make your own judgements.

OKAY, THAT'S a good overview of the four basic ingredients. Gather them together and have them ready. Also, planning for and gathering any enhancements or enrichments is a good idea. These could be written into the recipe, or they could spring free from your imagination.

ENHANCEMENTS & ENRICHMENTS

Everything that's not one of the basic core ingredients is an "enrichment" designed to enhance the flavor, the texture, or the look of the loaf. What kind and how much of each you use, and what enrichments you mix in, will be determined by the kind of bread you're making, the recipe, or by your own creativity.

There are really four kinds of enhancements, and most of the ingredients you can use will play into the dough in two or three ways at a time. (1) You can use structural enhancements, which will make the crumb more fluffy or more firm. (2) Enrichments do just as the name implies: they make the bread more rich. Describing that in words is difficult, but you probably get it. It's a deeper, more full flavor. Enrichments also add lots of calories, but who's counting? (3) Flavorings add, well, flavors on top of the baseline of the flour, yeast, and other enhancements. (4) Finally, textural enhancements will add crunch or other textures to the crumb or crust.

These enhancements are added into the dough itself, in the mixing stage, or in the kneading stage. Toppings are added on top of a shaped dough and are another topic.

OILS

Oils are basically an enrichment, but they can impact the crumb structure as well. They can lend a smoothness to the taste and the texture.

The oil I use the most is olive oil, because I like the subtle flavor. A lot of the breads I make are kinda based on European breads, French and Italian, so olive oil fits into those cuisines nicely.

On occasion, since it seemed cool, I've used flavored olive oils too. This is where you add herbs or spices to a jar of olive oil and let it set from several hours to several months. This infuses the flavors into the oil.

Vegetable oils are nice because they add that smoothness, but their flavor is even more neutral.

Butter adds a distinct flavor of its own, a richness that we all love. It's no surprise that we traditionally put butter on the bread, even when we don't put it in the bread. Butter can be up to 20 percent water, so keep that in mind as you're kneading the dough. Pay attention to the feel of the knead and adjust the added flour to maintain a good feel. I have found that when I use butter as an ingredient, the crumb turns out more dense and the flavor is more rich. For some reason, I tend to prefer this flavor in rolls, but it can be used in any shape.

I haven't used shortening in a yeast bread, but it could easily be added. It doesn't add any moisture to the mix, and it's flavor, like the vegetable oils, is more neutral. So this would be added primarily for the richness. I have used shortening quite often in quick breads, and it makes for a fluffy crumb.

Whichever oil you choose to use, a basic recipe would probably use about a tablespoon to a tablespoon and a half.

DAIRY

When I add dairy to a bread, it usually means milk. In addition to the deeper, richer flavor, milk also makes the crumb lighter and more fluffy.

I had been told that milk needs to be scalded before use in bread because it carries enzymes that can inhibit yeast growth. I was also told that using powdered milk would work as well. For some reason, however, I was having good success using unscalded milk. After a bit of research, I discovered the answer. It turns out that *raw* milk carries the enzyme. Pasteurized milk has already been scalded, so it's fine. That's actually one of the reasons why they say that raw milk is better for you. For drinking, that is. In breads, not so much.

When I make bread, I will often just pour the milk from the jug in the fridge. That works okay, but measuring it out beforehand would be better, as would letting it come up to room temperature—it's not really a big deal, but I get a better rise when I do this. Think of it: The warmer I can keep that doughball, the quicker and bigger it will rise. The same holds true of the eggs. And this is why you start out with water that's 110 degrees.

I'll usually use milk in a direct one-to-one substitution for water in the recipe. When a core recipe calls for two cups of liquid, I'll probably do one cup of water and one cup of milk.

Another dairy additive that I really like is plain yogurt. It not only adds fluffiness in the crumb, but it also brings a bit of tang to the flavor. It's still liquidy, so I use it as a substitute for water too, but not quite at one-to-one; I'll still leave a little extra water in the mix. By the end, you'll have adjusted the dryness/wetness of the dough by adding flour or not during kneading anyway. A few times I have wanted to use yogurt, but I didn't have any on hand, so I've used sour cream. The taste is good but not exactly the same as yogurt. When I've done it, I've measured it like yogurt.

For some real tang, try buttermilk. I usually use this more in quick breads, where the acid is needed to react with the baking soda or baking powder for chemical leavening. In fact, at first, I was nervous that the acid in buttermilk would inhibit yeast growth. Apparently not!

Cheese is, of course, a dairy product, but since it's usually a solid, it isn't going to contribute to the liquid in the recipe, and it won't impact the crumb structure much. Cheeses added into the body of the dough are more for flavor. It will work into the dough better if it's crumbled or grated, and about ¼ cup would be a good proportion to add to a basic core recipe.

EGG

There's really not much to say about eggs. I mean, it's not like there's a lot of variety. I guess you could try goose eggs, or quail eggs. . . .

The egg yolk adds richness and smoothness to the taste. The whites bond with the flour in cooking for extra structure and stability. It's like a double-whammy of goodness. Of course, an egg also adds fat, calories, and cholesterol. A single egg would be the right amount to add to a basic one-loaf recipe.

SWEETENERS

Sweeteners, like many of the other enhancements listed here, do double duty. In addition to adding flavor, they also help with the breadmaking process. Sweeteners give more for the yeast bugs to feed on, making the rise a little more energetic.

Most of the time, when I'm activating the yeast before mixing, I'll add some sweetener to the hot water, giving the yeast an even bigger head start. Sugar is the most common and readily accessible sweetener.

Brown sugar used to be what white sugar came from, but white sugar was farther down the process line. Now, brown sugar is generally white sugar with molasses added back into it. It has a slightly different flavor. If desired, try it in place of regular sugar.

Honey is my next sweetener of choice. In quantities under a cup, you can pretty much measure honey one-to-one against the sugar in a recipe. Darker honeys will have a stronger flavor than lighter honeys.

In the world of dark sweeteners, another one I like a lot is molasses. I often use it as much for the darkening color as for the flavor. It sweetens, true, but it also has a pungent punch to it, which I really like. In quantities like a basic one-loaf recipe, use only a tablespoon.

Agave nectar is like sugar and honey. It's supposed to flavor like them but be healthier, especially for diabetics. When I've cooked with it, I've substituted it one-to-one for the sugar.

I don't have any personal experience with any of the artificial, low- or no-calorie sweeteners. I don't know how the yeast would react with them. Most of the recipes I see that include them are cakes and things using a chemical leaven.

COLORINGS

The most obvious things to use for coloring are, of course, store-bought food colorings. You know, the ones you buy for eggs at Easter time? I would recommend using water-based colorings rather than oil or alcohol based (like the ones used for candies). Water-based colorings will be easier to blend in and mix. In all cases, a little goes a long way.

If you're wanting to mix the colors, I'd recommend blending them first and then pouring them into the dough before kneading. You could still make an adjustment of a drop or two in the kneading process.

If you're going for a swirled look, I recommend completely coloring and kneading two separate bread balls and then kneading and twisting them together briefly before the final proofing rise. I suppose you could put a few drops of different colors in different parts of the same doughball after the kneading was mostly complete. Then, a few more kneads would move the coloring around without blending them too much. You would also still have some of the basic white of the flour.

You can add in some other, more natural ingredients that will adjust the color. The colors won't be as deep or vivid as artificial colorings, but it will still add color and some unique flavors as well. You could tweak up a natural color with a bit of extra artificial color, if you wanted. Be careful. It could easily become unnatural.

If you're going for a red look, tomato paste adds a cool look and a unique taste in a bread. Add in about a six-ounce can for a basic loaf, and maybe back off the water just a bit. Some basil and oregano would make the bread an Italian treat! Another red could be made with a raspberry syrup or puree. Substitute an equal amount of the water in the recipe with the syrup or puree.

If you want to go dark, my favorite way is to use molasses instead of sugar. When I make the dark side of my swirled bread, I use a combination of molasses, cocoa, and Pero. Why not all three? For a basic loaf, I recommend a tablespoon of each. If you use the molasses in place of the sugar, use two tablespoons.

If you want a rich yellow, you could use Spanish saffron, but it's expensive, even though a little bit goes a long way. In a basic loaf, you could probably get some good color with ¼ teaspoon of saffron threads. Try it with a little lemon juice and/or zest in the bread too! For the richest color, grind up the saffron threads in a mortar and pestle or soak them in some of the warm water before mixing.

SEASONINGS AND HERBS

With so many possible combinations of spices, herbs, and seasonings, I can't possibly begin to cover them all. Look in your spice rack and see what you'd like to try. Even though some combinations will end up better than others, nothing is off-limits.

Because so many of the flavors found in spices, but also in herbs, are oils themselves, they tend to come out and be activated by oils. So shake a liberal amount of the seasoning into the two tablespoons of olive oil that you're going to add to the dough, and let it sit for an hour before you make your bread. In this situation, I recommend dried herbs rather than fresh.

Here are a few recommended combinations:

minced garlic, coarse ground pepper (not for everyone, but tasty)

parsley, thyme, oregano

cinnamon, nutmeg, cardamom, a little extra sugar

garlic, a titch of chili powder

Whenever you're messing with the flavor of the bread, you have to stop for a moment and think of what the bread will be paired with. A more neutral bread will be more adaptable, of course. A chili powder bread I made was great for savory meat sandwiches or as an accompaniment for a rich soup, but it wouldn't go so well for a PB&J.

Seasonings are added just for flavor, and they're not going to significantly impact the structure or the rising of the bread. Put in about a teaspoon of any one of these flavorings in a basic recipe. Less for stronger flavors, of course.

RAISINS, DRIED FRUIT, NUTS

Raisins, dried fruit, and nuts will add some flavor, but, more than that, they will add texture. In almost all cases of their use, I'll get out my chef's knife and chop these items up fairly coarsely. You're putting them in your bread because you want the chunks in there, but you also don't want the chunks to be so big as to be overpowering. Even things as small as raisins will at least get chopped in half or thirds before going into my breads. You can do whatever you like, though. Be creative!

STEP 2: PREFERMENT MIXING

Some kinds of breads require a preferment. This is usually mixing up half the dough and letting it rise for a time before mixing up the rest of the dough and letting it rise for real. Some of these preferments can be long, even overnight. They can often be goopy and runny too. When I make sourdough, I take my sourdough starter out of the fridge and activate it in some flour and water for an hour or two. Then I make a gloppy mix of flour and water called a "sponge," and I let that breed yeast germs overnight, sometimes in the fridge. French bread is made with a *pâte fermentée*, which is almost a firm dough in and of itself. Ciabatta and Focaccia loaves can start out as a "poolish," which is a runny starter.

These long rises, often chilled, give the yeast more time to convert the starches in the flour into sugars and to make the whole thing release its nutty tastes.

Most preferments I've used are the simplest of all. Usually it's flour, water, and yeast to get things going. The water doesn't even have to be any particular temperature since it often ends up in the fridge anyway.

If you do a preferment, make sure that the bowl you do it in is not made of metal (which reacts with the yeast), and make sure it's covered. Once I did a preferment and didn't cover it. It got this dried, chunky crust that I had to break up and pick out of the dough as I was kneading.

In most cases, when you're making a basic bread, you probably won't need a preferment. If that's the case, you'll skip this step and step three. The recipe will usually say if you need a preferment or not.

STEP 3: PREFERMENT RISE

This is one of the most enjoyable parts of breadmaking. Since I usually do preferments overnight, in the fridge, I'm usually asleep while it's happening. I like getting things done while I sleep!

Really, though, you're simply letting the yeast germs grow, divide, and burp out the CO_2. In the process, it develops more flavor. Not much to this step.

STEP 4: PRIMARY MIXING

Most people think of "making the bread" as starting with this phase, and the process pretty much does start here, unless you've done a preferment.

You might have to activate your yeast first if you don't have "instant yeast." To activate it, dissolve the yeast in some water that's about 110 degrees. Until I tested it on my own skin, I didn't really know what it was like. It turns out, it was hotter than I had thought when I'd read recipes that said "warm water." You have to be careful, however, because if the water is too hot, as in over 120 degrees, it can kill the yeast before it actually activates.

After about ten minutes or so in this almost-hot water, the yeast should be foaming up. I've had some success with yeasts that didn't foam up right away, but I can always tell it's gonna be a "good loaf day" when the yeast gets really foamy. It'll smell yeasty too.

If there's sugar or honey in the recipe, I'll sometimes include it with the water (which means I can make the water hotter). This helps wake up the yeast even more!

Following your recipe, mix up any of the dry ingredients. I've had a bit more success when I've sifted the flour. I haven't had problems with chunks in the flour, but sifting does aerate it, and it ends up a bit lighter in the crumb.

Also, If I'm working from a book, I begin with only about three-fourths of the flour that the recipe calls for. You never really know for sure exactly how much flour you'll need. Different flours from different bags, even on different days, will respond and absorb the liquid differently. I like to undershoot and add more in later.

Then, add in the wet ingredients and stir it all up. At this point, you're dealing with the yeast, so it should be in a nonmetallic bowl with a nonmetallic stirrer. The metal can react with the yeast. It doesn't make a huge difference, but I like to give the yeast bugs every chance I can.

STEP 5: KNEADING

For me, the kneading is usually a seamless extension of the mixing. Since I usually go a bit lower on the flour, the dough is usually wetter and stickier than it would be otherwise. Then I add in flour as I knead, and it will get to the right consistency.

I like mixing and kneading by hand rather than by machine. My wife makes delicious breads using the mixer, and they turn out great. But I like the feel of it in my fingers, and I can tell more easily when it's been kneaded enough.

Once the dough is basically stirred up in the bowl, I dump it out onto a liberally floured surface, like my countertop. At this point, the dough is probably pretty gooey, gloppy, and sticky. I shake some flour on top of it and just start rolling it and mashing it under my fingers and the heel of my hand. I press it, turn it, fold it over, and then do it again. It sticks to my hand and the countertop, so every so often I'll shake more flour on it and keep kneading.

I don't have any particular "correct" or "incorrect" techniques for kneading. I just work the dough. Sometimes, I'll use one hand, sometimes two. I do rotate the doughball on the tabletop a lot as I'm working it, to cover all the dough.

By gradually adding flour, I can get it to the right wetness. The easy way to tell is when it's consistently sticky enough to clean the dough from my hands, but not so sticky that it keeps leaving more. Usually, that means that I use slightly less flour than most recipes call for. I'm okay with that; I think it makes for a more fluffy crumb.

If you don't knead enough, then the gluten will be underdeveloped and won't have the structure to trap the gas from the yeast. The dough won't rise enough, and it will end up dense.

Most recipes will say to knead for a certain length of time. I gave up on that method because I was never getting it long enough. I use the windowpane test to determine how long to knead. I cut off a chunk and make a ball about the size of a golf ball. I start working it in my fingers, flatter and flatter, and stretching it out. If I can stretch it to a thin, translucent windowpane, before it tears, then the gluten is sufficiently developed and I'm done kneading. If it tears before that point, it's not ready, and I need to keep kneading. Eventually, as you keep making bread, you'll get to the point where you'll be able to tell when it's ready by the way it feels in your fingers.

When the dough is ready after kneading, form it into a ball, stretching the upper surface of the dough and tucking it underneath. This will create a nice, tight skin. Spray the bowl you mixed it in with oil and set the ball in, tucked side down. Spray a layer of oil over the ball and cover it with a towel or plastic wrap so it doesn't dry out.

One fun way to make that surface nice and tight is to put the doughball on the table, with no flour, and to cover the ball loosely in your hands. Sweep your hands in a circle on the tabletop, without exerting pressure on the dough. The tabletop will grab onto the bottom of the dough and pull it into the center of the ball, tightening the skin on top.

STEP 6: PRIMARY RISE

The next step is to set it aside to rise. I have two possibilities for you, and which one you choose will be determined largely by your circumstances.

First, there's the warm rise. This is where you leave the dough out on your countertop or any other warm environment. Yeast grows best at 80–100 degrees. In my experience, this will mean that a typical ball of yeast will be risen and ready to go in 1–2 hours. A typical room temperature of my house is around the mid-70s, so my rising time will be closer to the 2-hour mark. The timing on the rising is more critical with this method, and I've had some loaves that didn't turn out as well because I over- or under-raised them.

Second, there's the cold rise. This is where you put the dough in the fridge and let it rise there. Since the fridge isn't the optimal temperature for yeast production, the dough will rise much more slowly. A slow rise gives several advantages. First of all, the timing of the steps are more drawn out and much more adaptable and forgiving. For example, much of my baking is done on Sunday. Doing a cold rise allows me to mix and knead in the morning. I'll let it start rising in the morning too, and then it will continue to rise while I'm in church. When I come home, I can take it out to warm up, and I can take my time getting ready to bake it. Since the overall rise takes longer, the window of opportunity when the dough is ready to be shaped is wider as well. A cold rise also gives a more rich and complex flavor, since the fermentation is taking longer.

Of course, if you're in a hurry, you'll do the warm rise.

STEP 7: DEGASSING (PUNCHDOWN) AND SHAPING

This step has always made me nervous. Remember that quote at the beginning, in the introduction? This is where the magic starts to come together.

If I've used the right flour, *if* I kneaded correctly, and *if* the yeast was good and active, then I'll be able to punch down the growing doughball and shape it, and it will continue to rise. On many occasions, those stars didn't align, and after punching down (also called "degassing") and shaping, the dough didn't rise any more. So I'm always nervous at this part. Still, if you've taken care of business up to this point, everything should work out.

Simply punch your fist into the dough to break up some of the gas bubbles and knead it again for a couple of strokes. This will redistribute the ingredients a little bit and allow the yeast to encounter fresh food.

If it's a wetter, more rustic bread, then don't handle it as much in the degassing. You'll want to keep as much of that initial CO_2 as possible in place. Firmer, drier breads can handle the additional rise.

At this point, the bread could be shaped into any number of forms for baking. You need to decide at this stage because the shape you choose could determine how you go about preheating the Dutch oven in the next step.

In one scenario, you shape the dough and set it aside in a basket, in a bowl, or on parchment or cloth to have a final rise, called proofing. While this is happening, preheat the entire Dutch oven, top and bottom. Usually, I prefer this method because the bread bakes more consistently top to bottom. This scenario works well with the large boule or hearth loaves.

The other scenario has you shaping the dough and setting it into an oiled, cool Dutch oven pan. The bread dough proofs in the bottom of the Dutch oven, while the oven lid preheats separately with lots of coals on top. This is done when the shape of the dough makes it so that you can't easily transfer it. Rolls, for example, would be difficult to immediately transfer from proofing to heated pot. A coil or a curved braid would be done best as a "pot proof" with a preheated lid.

You need to decide which process you're going to do in this stage so that you can properly prepare the oven and properly proof the dough.

Here are some shapes I like:

The easiest to do in a Dutch oven is the boule, or ball. This will also give you a good hearth loaf. Simply stretch the top of the dough again, tuck it under the bottom of the dough, and pinch it closed.

I'll usually set the dough to rest on a piece of parchment paper or a tea towel, to be placed in a fully preheated Dutch oven later. Recently I acquired a couple of cloth-covered baskets that I use. A hint: Place the boule in the basket pinched side (bottom) up. That way, when you upend it into the Dutch oven, the smooth, tight surface comes out on top. Also, even if the pinch breaks open, it will become the bottom crust anyway.

A variant of this shape is what I call the "quarter boule." This is done by cutting the dough into quarters and forming each piece into a smaller boule. These can be set immediately into an oiled Dutch oven or set on parchment or cloth to be lifted later into a preheated oven. They don't work as well in the baskets. I usually do these as a pot proof with a preheated lid. They bake into circular triangles, which cut nicely into sandwich slices. They also easily break apart so you can give them to neighbors.

Another common shape is rolls. Cut the ball into a dozen or so equal chunks and shape them into tiny boules using the same tuck-and-pinch technique. Place these in an oiled Dutch oven for the second rise.

Rounds and braids are shapes that I like a lot. They look cool coming out of the Dutch oven (especially braids)! Roll out a long log of dough or make a long braid from three logs. Pinch the ends together and set it in a circle in the oiled Dutch oven. Again, we'll preheat the oven lid later.

A bâtard is a long, narrow loaf, somewhere in between a boule and a thin baguette. It's the traditional shape of a French bread loaf, and to bake it you need a cast-iron oval roaster. This functions much like a Dutch oven, but it's oblong. To make this shape, stretch a boule out long and then stretch the top under and pinch it, keeping the long shape. Let it proof on cloth or parchment and then lower it gently into a fully preheated oven.

You can choose from so many shapes for so many breads, and I would encourage you to try them all. Experiment!

STEP 8: PREPARING THE DUTCH OVEN

As soon as I've set the dough to proof (the second rise), I light the coals for my Dutch oven. I recommend lighting up 35–40 coals. This will leave you some extras for lighting more coals in case the bread takes longer to bake. The coals will take (under most circumstances) about 15–20 minutes to show some good white ash.

If you're doing a full top and bottom preheat, take a minute to oil the inside of the Dutch oven. Use any kind of oil you want, but don't make it heavy. A quick spray with cooking spray works well, or do a light brushing with veggie oil on a paper towel. This will also help build up your black pot's patina, by the way, because it will bake on while the bread bakes.

Once the coals are showing some heat (the edges are turning white), it's time to preheat either the oven or the lid. If your dough is proofing on parchment, on a cloth, in a basket, or on the tabletop, then you can heat the entire Dutch oven. If the dough is proofing in the Dutch oven, you'll have to make do with preheating the lid.

To preheat the whole oven, make a ring of coals, with each coal touching, underneath the oven. That will probably be 12–14 coals for a 12-inch Dutch oven (use the recipe as a guide). Make another ring of touching coals on the lid and place it on the oven. This will be about 16–20 coals for a 12-inch Dutch oven. The target internal temperature is between 400 and 450 degrees. Sometimes, if I'm thinking ahead, I'll actually put an oven thermometer in the base of the empty Dutch oven to gauge the rising temperature.

To preheat the lid, place one ring of coals (as described above) around the outer rim of the lid and add 6–8 extra coals in the center of the lid. I usually set it on a lid stand off to the side of where I'm going to do the baking. When the time comes to set up the bottom coals, you can take some from the preheating lid.

Whether you're heating the lid or the whole oven, it will usually take about 15 minutes to get the iron hot enough. At that point you're ready to bake.

But before we go to that, let's rewind time for a moment and talk about what's happening with the dough while we're getting the heat ready.

STEP 9: SECOND RISE/PROOFING

Basically, all this time, while the coals and the oven are heating up, the dough is rising again. It's going through a second fermentation (or, technically, a third, if you used a preferment). You don't need this rising to be as extensive as the first one. It doesn't need to double in bulk again, but it will still need to noticeably swell.

Toward the end of this proofing, you can also coat the dough with things to make the crust more tasty, colorful, or decorative. Let's talk about options for toppings.

TOPPINGS

Putting on a topping is another great way to add variety to your breads. These can be ingredients that are spread or rolled on top of your dough before, during, or even after the baking. Your options are as varied as the choices for enhancements in the dough itself. Here are some suggestions.

EGG

I love putting an egg wash on the top of my loaves because it gives the finished bread a rich brown shine. I crack an egg into a small bowl and whisk it thoroughly. I wash it onto the top of the dough with a basting brush right before I slice the top and put on the Dutch oven lid. If I'm doing a pot proof, I can do the egg wash a little earlier, but I like the look of it best when the slice happens last. Then the dough opens and parts all of the other toppings.

An egg wash is also a great glue to attach other toppings, like seeds or other shapes of bread, into place. Be careful: If the egg wash runs down under the loaf or between the loaf and the walls of the Dutch oven, the bread will stick to the oven after baking. When I use a wash, I'll usually run a knife around the edge of the Dutch oven, between it and the bread after it bakes, when I'm about to remove the loaf.

BUTTER

Butter melting onto the bread will infuse the loaf with a rich flavor. It will also soften the crust. Sometimes I'll simply smear some butter onto the hot crust after the bread comes out of the oven and let the butter melt into the crust!

MILK

Milk will help with browning and softening the crust. It also gives a subtle sweetness to the crust. Sometimes, I'll wash with milk and then sprinkle with sugar or brown sugar, creating a sweet crunch on top.

CHEESE

A baked-on cheese can add flavor and crunch to the final product, but it can be tricky. Soft cheeses like mozzarella or cheddar on top of a regular loaf (not a flat dough, like pizza) can burn if they're added right before baking. In those cases, I add them during baking, when I check the bread and add the thermometer after the first turn.

Hard grated cheeses, like Parmesan or myzithra, can go on before baking. Using some oil or water to help them stay on can be a good idea too.

SEEDS/HERBS/SEASONINGS

If you've used any seasonings as enrichments in the dough, using the same things as toppings, or even something complementary, can be cool. Just before the final proof, wet the top of the dough with a brush or spray—with water, milk, or egg—and then roll the dough in the topping. You can sprinkle it on as well, but rolling it presses the topping into the dough surface and makes it adhere better, especially after the baking. Then let the dough proof with the topping up, and score and bake it as normal.

GLAZES

A glaze is a thick, usually sweet coating on top that bakes into the upper crust. A simple glaze would be ¼ cup of brown sugar with enough milk to make a slightly runny paste. Honey and spices make a great glaze too.

One of my favorite glazes:

¼ cup orange juice concentrate

¼ cup brown sugar

cinnamon

nutmeg

orange zest

a little orange juice, fresh squeezed, to make the right consistency

I've found that glazes work best when spread on in the last half of baking. There's less chance of them burning that way. You'll also have to be careful when removing the loaf from the Dutch oven, because the sugars can glue the loaf to the pot.

FLOUR

Dusting with flour after proofing and before scoring produces a really cool rustic look to a hearth loaf. One cool trick I've seen is to create a stencil design, like an initial monogram or a logo, out of paper. Hold the stencil over the loaf when you're dusting it, creating the pattern in flour, which then bakes into place.

CORNMEAL

Here's an interesting story about cornmeal and wheat flour bread baking. I've heard a lot of stories why this is added (usually to the bottom crust): the flavor, the texture, the crunch, the rustic look . . .

I learned about the origins of the practice when I worked in a pizza house. When any dough is shaped, the standard practice is to use flour to keep it from sticking to everything while it's being worked into shape, right? The problem was that in professional bakeries, a lot of flour was flying around as bakers shaped their dough. The bakers breathed in all of that flour flying around, and it wasn't healthy. So they started using cornmeal to dust the tabletops for dough shaping. Cornmeal is more coarse and is heavier, so it doesn't fly up into the air.

I guess people liked it because the practice has caught on, and now even home bakers are using cornmeal, even though they're not really at risk for breathing in flour day in and day out.

At any rate, cornmeal does create a nice texture on a crust, particularly a bottom crust. Simply press the dough bottom onto cornmeal spread over your tabletop before proofing.

STEP 10: BAKING/PARBAKING

Once the Dutch oven or the lid is sufficiently heated, it's time to bake.

If you've done a pot proof, the process is pretty simple. Grab your razor blade and slice the top of the dough. This will allow it to spring more in the initial heat and will also vent some of the steam inside. There are many ways you can slash, and some of the options will be determined by the shape. A bâtard is traditionally slashed in 2–3 diagonals. A boule can be slashed with 2–3 parallel lines, a cross or plus sign across the center, or even a spiral radiating out from the center. Use your creativity!

Use a razor and not a kitchen knife. I've found that only razor blades are sharp enough to effectively cut the dough. All other knives will grab and tear the dough.

If you like, you can gently mist the surface of the dough with water. This will make for a thicker, crustier bread. Do this immediately before applying the heat.

With the proofed bread in it, set the Dutch oven on a ring of coals. Then put the preheated lid on, with the proper number of coals on it. Mark the time, and take a deep breath!

If you've been preheating the entire oven, then the transfer process is a little trickier. It has to happen fast so you lose as little interior heat as possible. Gather together everything you'll need around you at the cooking station. It's a bit of mise en place. You'll need the shaped dough, a razor, a thermometer (for later), and an optional spray bottle of water. Decide in advance how you're going to slice it and whether or not you want to spritz.

Move quickly: Lift the lid. Place the dough. Slice the dough. Spritz the dough. Close the lid.

If you're using parchment paper, simply lift it with the dough into the Dutch oven. Let it sit in the oven the entire time it bakes. If it's been proofing on a cloth, gently roll it off the cloth into the oven. If it was in a basket, hold the basket over the center of the oven and turn it over. In general, you want to do what will degas the least. When the bread hits the oven, it will probably sizzle a little right away. Not to worry. Your bottom crust will be fine!

Again, mark the time and take a deep breath!

About 15 minutes later, turn the oven. Lift it up off the bottom coals (tap the coals to shake off the ash that's built up) and rotate the oven about a quarter turn. Then turn the lid about a quarter turn. It doesn't matter which direction you do the turns. The idea is to put the bread in a different place in relation to the coals, which prevents the dough being overcooked in one area due to a hot spot on the oven.

At this point, I usually lift the lid quickly to check on the bread. I'll also insert the short-probe thermometer. I won't look at it long; I open the Dutch oven, check the bread, place the thermometer, and close the oven back up.

It may be necessary to add more coals as they burn down. Don't add too many coals—just enough so that it feels like the heat is constant. A few on the bottom and a few on the top. If it's cold out, keep the oven hotter. The best way to judge is practice. I wish I could specify with more clarity and detail, but there are too many variables.

In most cases, I don't need to refresh any coals. If I let the coals burn down, the bread will be done before they go out. The coals have a natural tendency to gradually lower the heat a bit. That helps the bread cook better. Sometimes, however, if there's a stiff breeze, the coals will burn faster, and I'll replenish.

Telling when the bread is done in a Dutch oven is difficult. Because of the many variations in heat, just looking at the color of the crust won't tell you anything, and lifting the bread out and thumping the bottom isn't practical. So, after a couple of turns, or a total of 30–40 minutes for most breads, check the thermometer. We'll be shooting for an internal temperature of between 190 degrees (for lighter breads) and 210 degrees (for denser, crustier breads, like rye or whole wheat).

In addition, if you pull the thermometer out and it's pretty much clean, then that's a good sign that the bread is done.

When the bread's done, I shake the coals off the lid (away from the bread so it doesn't get ash all over) and take the oven off the bottom coals. I shake, lift, or dump the bread out (using hot pads or oven mitts) and set it to cool on an oven rack.

I need to say a bit about parbaking. Technically, parbaking would happen before the regular bake, so I could have mentioned it earlier, but it's rare in the home baking world, so I'll cover it here. Parbaking is when the dough is precooked a bit before the final bake. This is done often in bakeries and restaurants so the partially cooked dough can be stored and, just before selling or serving, baked and browned for real.

Parbaking also has a few other applications, such as boiling pretzels or bagels in a special solution to get that shiny gloss with the chewy dough. Then they're baked for the final browning and setting of the crumb. The bottom crust of a deep-dish Chicago-style pizza has to carry a lot of weight. Parbaking it first preserves its own airiness. Then, once the toppings and upper crust are in place, the final bake is done.

STEP 11: COOLING

When I first started baking bread, I was always nervous about the bread being done enough or about it being too doughy. I would cut it open right away to check. I was often disappointed because it wasn't finished inside.

Allowing the bread to cool sufficiently is important. Not only does it keep you from being burned, but cooling is actually the final stage in the cooking process. I didn't realize this before. No wonder the bread always looked a little underdone! I also used to let the bread cool in the Dutch oven, but I don't anymore. If all that steam gets trapped underneath the bread, the bottom crust will get soggy. Not softer, but soggier.

Some people say to let the bread cool to room temperature, but I'm usually too impatient. I like melting butter and honey on freshly baked bread. Still, you have to let it cool almost completely or it won't be fully cooked.

I've also noticed that the steam and moisture escaping during the cooling process makes the crust a bit softer. It might look quite hard as it comes out of the oven, but it will soften as it cools. Passing a knife-ful of butter over it while it's still hot will help that too!

STEP 12: EATING/ SHARING/STORING

This is the best part, and it doesn't need much explanation!

Dig in and enjoy. I always try a slice or so of my loaves without any toppings or sandwich things. I do love butter and honey, but first, I want to taste the bread itself and see how it compares to the last loaf I did. How did the enrichments add to and complement the taste of the crumb itself? How was the caramelization of the crust? I want to get to know that loaf's flavor before I go mixing it up with cheese, meats, or jelly!

In our house, we go through bread fairly quickly, be it homemade or commercial. Still, we keep it on the countertop in plastic, which can trap the moisture. On the one hand, this means it won't dry out as quick. On the other hand, it will get moldy quicker. Also, plastic can act as a sort of greenhouse and draw the bread's moisture to the surface, creating soggy spots.

Paper bags protect the freshness for a while, but the moisture will escape and the bread will dry out. Putting bread in the fridge can keep it fresh longer, but then it's cooler, and I like to eat my bread at room temperature.

Bread can be frozen, and I recommend freezing it in plastic bags. Then when you're ready to eat it, bring it out and let it thaw in the air, not in the microwave.

A word about sharing too: Do it!

When I was a young man, barely six months married and moving into my first house, a neighbor came over with a loaf of fresh bread his wife had just baked. He and I grew to become close friends over the years that we lived there. I've never forgotten his kindness, and I try to pay it forward whenever I can. Cookies at Christmas and cakes for birthdays and neighborhood parties are great, but a fresh loaf of bread as a between-holiday surprise can set a friendship just like the baking sets the dough!

THAT'S MY 12-step Dutch oven breadmaking process. Each bread recipe will follow this basic process, but not every recipe will utilize all 12. The better you understand how all the steps work together to make tasty, chewy, crusty breads, the better baker you'll be!

In the next few chapters, let me share some of my favorite recipes with you!

Chapter 4
Common Breads

NOW THAT we've had a lot of theory and process, I've chosen some of the many recipes and stories from the "pages" of my blog, marksblackpot.com. Since these are from all across the spectrum of my learning process, I've updated and edited a few of them to reflect the results of my journey.

Also, since the recipes are all for breads, many of the processes are similar. I've repeated the description of the process so that if someone were to want to simply look up a recipe they would have it all in front of them. This may mean that, for the start-to-finish reader, you'll find a lot of repetitive spots. Sorry.

This first set of breads are all the sort of things that go well with everyday sandwiches, meals, and general eating. They're not what I consider fancier or more complex breads. I still like them lots, though.

SANDWICH BREAD

Okay, so I've done sourdoughs and ryes and all kinds of "hearth breads"— the crusts are often "crustier," and the crumbs are more dense. That's not bad when you want a hearty chunk of bread for a meat-based sandwich. But I also wanted to learn how to make something light. I wanted something I can make a PB&J on and have my kids eagerly eat it.

Here's a great recipe, full of enrichments, that makes a delicious, sweet, and fluffy bread. It's wonderful for sandwiches. My dear wife has made this one for years, and it's one of the first ones I was able to pull off successfully in a Dutch oven.

Jodi's Bread in the Dutch Oven

TOOLS

12-inch Dutch oven

10–12 coals below

18–20 coals above

INGREDIENTS

1 Tbsp. yeast

1 cup hot water

¾ cup honey

4–5 cups flour, plus about 1 cup to be added during kneading

a pinch of salt

1 egg

1 cup milk

2 Tbsp. oil

1 egg, to coat the top

I start by activating the yeast. I mix the hot water and the honey (which cools the water but not enough for it to be cool). Then I add the yeast. I set the mixture aside in a plastic or ceramic mixing bowl to proof and grow. Then I gather up all the other ingredients except the egg for coating. I mix in the flour and the salt first, followed by the other wet ingredients. Then I add the yeast mixture. I stir it all up with my trusty wooden spoon and then dump the dough out onto a floured tabletop. I begin kneading, adding more flour as I do. This recipe usually passes the windowpane test quickly, in only about 10–15 minutes of kneading. When I've kneaded enough, the dough is stiffer also.

Then I put the dough in a bowl that's been lightly misted with spray oil. I also spray the dough with oil and then cover it with plastic wrap. I let it rise up for a little over an hour.

When that is done, I punch the dough down and divide it and shape it into four doughballs, like loaves, and set them in the Dutch oven to proof.

Since this is a pot proof, I light up the coals. When they're glowing and white, I put them on the lid to preheat. While it's preheating, I beat up the extra egg and coat it on the top of the dough loaves with a basting brush. Then I slice the tops of each small loaf. After the lid has had 15 minutes or so with the coals on it, I reset the coals to be under and above, according to the numbers on the previous page, and I put the lid on. I let the bread bake for 15 minutes. Then I turn the Dutch oven and check it. I usually put in the thermometer then too. Another 15–20 minutes and it's usually done. If not, I may replenish 3–4 coals below and 5–6 coals above.

When the bread loaves are done and I pull them out, I make sure the crumb inside is cooked all the way through and is nice and soft, not doughy at all. The crust is often dark but still soft to the bite. I leave the loaves to cool on a cooling rack, and they are ready in about an hour!

Having the four quarter loaves makes it easy to divide, slice, store in baggies, and share. Now, where's the butter and honey?

WHOLE WHEAT BREAD

When I was growing up, my mom would often bake this delicious whole-wheat bread. It was wonderful and hearty. As I started to focus my learning on breads, I wanted to go back and make this bread as well, in the Dutch oven. I went to my sister for the recipe, and here it is!

It turns out that this bread is actually a part wheat, part white dough, about 70/30 split. The white flour makes the bread a little lighter, but it also gives more gluten to help the dough rise; whole-wheat dough doesn't create much gluten on its own. This recipe also adds more in the form of gluten powder.

This is the story of the first time I made it:

Mark's Family's Whole-Wheat Bread

TOOLS

12-inch Dutch oven

12 coals below

22–24 coals above

INGREDIENTS

The basic flour mix:

- 3 cups white bread flour
- 6 cups whole-wheat flour
- ¼ cup vital wheat gluten
- 3 Tbsp. dough enhancer (optional)

The wet mix:

- 2 cups milk
- ⅓ cup honey
- 1 Tbsp. yeast
- 2 eggs
- ⅓ cup oil

The first thing I did was to make the flour mix. It's pretty simple: add the ingredients and stir it up. You won't need this much flour mix, but it's good to have extra for next time. (I used whole-wheat flour that was ground for us by Jodi's stepdad. He had found an old electric grinder, fixed it up, and made this huge bucket of flour for us. So this really is a big family thing! This bread is delicious with freshly ground flour.)

Then, I made the wet mix in a different bowl. I heated the milk, added the honey, let it dissolve, and waited until the milk cooled to about the temperature of a hot bath. I added the yeast, stirred it to dissolve it, and let it bubble.

When it had bubbled up well, I added the eggs and the oil and whisked that all together.

Then, in the same bowl, I started adding the flour mix. The last time I'd done this, I went too fast, and it ended up too dry. Adding moisture while you're kneading isn't easy. It's much easier to add the flour slowly and sneak up on the right amount.

I added the flour in the bowl for the first few cups, stirring as I went with a wooden spoon. Once it got to the point where it was pulling from the sides, but still quite messy, I dumped it onto a generously floured table and started kneading, slowly adding more flour as needed.

Kneading whole-wheat dough is a workout. I seriously kneaded for a full half hour before I got a good windowpane stretch going on. I think in future batches I might add even more gluten flour in the mix.

Finally, I was done kneading, and I set it aside to rise. It rose well. At that point, I punched it down and rolled it into a boule loaf. I've tried a double boule with this same recipe, and I've also done it with quarter loaves like the previous recipe.

As soon as I set the shaped loaf aside to proof, I started the coals to preheat the oven. Once the coals were getting white, I set the oven on them, with the right count on the lid, for about 15 minutes.

Once the loaf had proofed and the oven was hot, I put the loaf in. I baked it, turning at 15 minutes and replenishing the coals as needed. I baked it to an internal temperature of about 200 degrees.

The loaf didn't spring in the oven as much as white bread does. At first, that made me think that something had gone wrong, but that's just how it happens with whole wheat. It's a heavier, denser dough, so it has a heavier, denser crumb. Once the loaf is out and cooling, rub a stick of butter over the top, which will soften the crust a little bit as well as impart a delicious flavor! Mom always used to do that.

General Conference Cinnamon Rolls

Twice a year, our church has a big meeting out of the central offices in Salt Lake City, Utah. It's called "general conference." In five two-hour sessions over two days, the Church leaders talk on a variety of topics. It's broadcast all over the world, even via the Internet.

When I was a kid, we watched it on TV, and in the morning, Mom would make some kind of sweet bread with us, usually cinnamon rolls, to help us keep our little hands busy while we listened to the conference.

So I decided to relive and revive our old family tradition of making sweet cinnamon rolls in my Dutch ovens on conference Saturday.

TOOLS

12-inch Dutch oven

10–12 coals below

18–22 coals above

INGREDIENTS

1 Tbsp. dry yeast

½ cup warm water

½ cup warm milk

⅓ cup sugar

⅓ cup shortening

1 tsp. salt

1 egg

3–4 cups flour

2 Tbsp. softened butter

2 tsp. ground cinnamon

¼ cup sugar

a few shakes of ground ginger

a small handful of brown sugar

I got up early to start this off. I let the yeast activate and foam up in the water. I added all the ingredients in the second set (except the flour) and mixed all that up. Then I started adding in the flour, a cup or two at a time. I don't remember exactly how many cups it took for me this time.

Then I started kneading the dough on the table. I added shakes of flour onto the table as I went along. This time, as with the last time I made a yeast bread, I kneaded the dough until I felt it loosen up. I also used the windowpane test. Kneading took 8–10 minutes. Then I set it aside to rise.

It rose slowly and took about an hour and a half to double in size. Once it had doubled, I put it back on the floured tabletop and rolled it out flat, into a square (or as close to a square as I could get). I spread the butter over the surface and then sprinkled it with a mix of cinnamon, sugar, and ginger (we actually had some already mixed).

Then I rolled the dough up like a log and sliced it into one-inch lengths. I set these into an oiled Dutch oven. Once all the rolls were in the oven, I set them aside to proof. That took about 40 minutes. Then I sprinkled the brown sugar over the tops of the raised rolls and then shook some more ground ginger on top of that—not much, though. While the dough was proofing, I lit the coals, got them white, and preheated the lid.

I set up the Dutch oven on and under the coals and let it bake for about 40 minutes. When the rolls were all done and cooled, they were delicious!

Monkey Bread

One year at Easter time, we were invited up to a friend's home for an Easter party. I thought about making sweet rolls, but since there would be a lot of people there, I thought it would be better to make monkey bread. That's basically the same thing as a cinnamon roll, but it's smaller, so more people can get a portion.

Many people make monkey bread by taking canned "pop up" biscuits and rolling them in cinnamon sugar. Then you stack them randomly in your Dutch oven and bake them. That's easy enough, but I love making things from scratch, so I jumped in and did it. I also love yeast bread, so I did it that way.

TOOLS

12-inch Dutch oven

10–12 coals below

20–24 coals above

INGREDIENTS

2 Tbsp. yeast

2 cups warm water

¾ cup sugar

5–6 cups flour

1½ tsp. salt

1 cup butter

2 eggs

some sugar

2 Tbsp. ground cinnamon

First, I activated the yeast by stirring it into the water in a cup. While that was getting all bubbly, I mixed the sugar, flour, and salt in a bowl, but only about 4 cups of the flour to start. I sifted the flour. I've gotten into the habit of doing that. It aerates the flour and makes it a bit lighter as a result.

Then I cut in the butter with my pastry cutter. I guess another option would be to melt the butter into the powders. Either way.

I added the eggs and the yeast mixture to the bowl. I stirred it all together, turned the dough out onto the floured countertop, and kneaded until I got a good windowpane. Once it was all kneaded, I set it aside to rise.

In about 2 hours, it had risen nicely. I mixed some sugar into the cinnamon until it looked like a nice blend and it tasted right. I started pinching off doughballs that were about the size of Ping-Pong balls, rolled them in the cinnamon/sugar mixture, and put them into the oiled Dutch oven. I didn't worry much about the placement; I simply scattered them evenly. After putting them in, I sprinkled the rest of the cinnamon/sugar over the top.

Once the doughballs were made, I started up some coals, and when those were getting white, I put 25–30 of them on the lid of the Dutch oven to preheat. That was heating while the dough was rising a second time in the body of the Dutch oven. Once they both were ready, I put the Dutch oven on and under the right amount of coals and baked them for about an hour. I used the thermometer and got them to 190–200 degrees.

Sometimes when I do this, the bread burns a little on top. I'm sure that it's a combination of the blast of upper heat from the lid and the sugar sprinkled on top. Later in the bake time, you can remove some of the upper coals.

Since I'm not worried about a lower crust, I let these cool in the Dutch oven. They were sure yummy, and everyone at the party loved them.

Amazing Rolls

I made these rolls when I was preparing to do my first Dutch oven cook-off. They accompanied my salmon-and-rice dish. I placed fourth out of eight, so that's not bad, right? This is a rich dough, and it makes the crumb a little dense, but it is also flavorful.

TOOLS

12-inch Dutch oven (I used my deep one)

10 coals below

20 coals above

INGREDIENTS

1 Tbsp. yeast

½ cup warm water

1 cup melted butter (melt a half cup first, then another half later on)

2 eggs

½ cup sugar

1 cup milk

5+ cups flour

1 tsp. salt

I started by mixing the yeast and the water and letting it stand for 15 minutes or so, to activate the yeast and foam up. Then, in my mixing bowl, I added ½ cup of melted butter, the eggs, and the sugar. Then I added the milk, stirred it all up, and then added the yeast and water.

Next I added 5 cups of flour and the salt, stirring as I went, to make a smooth doughball. I turned it out onto the countertop and kneaded it, adding more flour as necessary. I worked it until it was able to stretch thin, for the windowpane test.

I put the dough back in the mixing bowl and then covered the dough with a damp cloth and set the bowl somewhere warm (in the summer I use the back porch) for a couple of hours. (At the cook-off, I started with the bread, to allow for lots of rising time.) I let the doughball double in bulk.

I broke off chunks somewhere between the size of a golf ball and a tennis ball and arranged them in the bottom of the greased Dutch oven. Then I spread the other ½ cup of melted butter liberally over the doughballs with a basting brush.

Now, when I baked these at the cook-off, I simply put the coals under the oven and on top of the lid. It baked up okay, but now I recommend preheating the lid with lots of coals for 15 minutes or so before setting up the listed amount of coals.

Let the dough bake for 15–20 minutes and then turn the lid a quarter turn. Turn the oven a quarter turn as well. Insert a thermometer into the roll dough at that point too. Bake until the internal temperature is 190 degrees, which will take about 1 hour.

The tricky part about baking, as always, is heat management. The oven needs to be hot, but if it's too hot, the bread burns above and below and is still doughy in the middle. If the oven isn't hot enough, the bread never cooks at all. The sad thing is, I don't think you can learn how to regulate heat by reading a book or a blog. The only way is to try it on your own, following the directions as close as you can, and then see if it works. Making good bread in a Dutch oven took me many tries. Fortunately, this recipe was one of the winners!

Quick Parmesan Breadsticks

Once, I was making this pasta dish, and Jodi thought it would be good with some breadsticks. She showed me this recipe in an old neighborhood cookbook. I admit I was a bit skeptical. It was a yeast bread recipe, but the rise time was short and the instructions were strange. But I decided to give it a shot.

TOOLS

12-inch Dutch oven

12 coals below

22 coals above

INGREDIENTS

1½ cups warm water

1 Tbsp. yeast

1 Tbsp. honey

1 tsp. salt

about 4 cups flour

¼ cup melted butter

liberal shakes of parmesan cheese and other seasonings

First, in a bowl, I put the water, yeast, and honey together and let the yeast activate. Then I added the salt and the flour. I didn't add the flour all at once, because I wanted to gauge the moistness and the density of the dough when kneading. I kneaded it for 10 minutes, and then I let it sit for about a half hour. This wasn't so much to let the dough rise as to let the gluten relax after kneading.

Then I poured the melted butter in the bottom of the Dutch oven and spread the dough out over it. I cut the dough into strips. Then I sprinkled on the parmesan and the seasonings (I used this really great salad seasoning combo). This is where I was skeptical with the original recipe. At that point, I set it aside for about 30–40 minutes to rise. That's it. No long rise or proofing. While it was rising, I got the coals ready and preheated the lid of the Dutch oven, for at least 15 minutes

Finally, once the dough had risen some, I put the Dutch oven on the coals. In 20–30 minutes, the breadsticks were done. And they were delicious!

Chapter 5
Ethnic Breads

I GUESS I should title this chapter "Breads from Other Countries." I mean, what does "ethnic" really mean? And most of these breads have been baked here in America so often that they're not really "from" the country in their name anymore.

But anyway, here are some great recipes!

(Like I mentioned in the last chapter, if you're reading along, you'll see a lot of repetition, especially in the procedures. That's so those who look up a recipe can know how to make it.)

Italian Bread

A lot of European breads involve preferments of some kind. These have many different names, like starter, poolish, biga, or sponge. Really, all it means is that there is a step before the main mixing and kneading that involves fermentation and rising. This helps develop more flavor in the dough. Typically, these breads have fewer flavoring enrichments and rely more on the basic flour, water, yeast, and salt.

INGREDIENTS: THE BIGA

2½ cups unbleached bread flour

½ tsp. yeast

¾–1 cup water, room temperature

I mixed the ingredients in a bowl and then turned it out onto a floured tabletop and kneaded for a few minutes until it all came together. At this stage, I didn't worry much about it forming a windowpane. I simply wanted it to feel smooth, like a bread dough in and of itself. Then I oiled it and put plastic wrap over it in a bowl, which I put in the fridge overnight.

If it hadn't been so late at night when I made the biga, I actually would have set it out to rise for a couple of hours and then put it in the fridge.

The next morning, I took the it out of the fridge and set it out to come back up to room temperature. At that point, I chopped it up into about 10 pieces. Then I gathered the ingredients for the main dough mix.

INGREDIENTS: THE MAIN DOUGH

3½ cups biga (pretty much all of what I mixed the night before)

2½ cups unbleached bread flour

1⅔ tsp. salt

1 Tbsp. sugar

1 tsp. yeast

1 Tbsp. olive oil

¾ cup water, at about 100 degrees

I mixed all of the ingredients in a bowl and then dumped it out on the floured counter and began kneading for real. I kneaded for almost 20 minutes, and at that point I got a good windowpane. I set that aside to rise on the countertop.

This time, it rose quite well. After only about 2 hours, it was ready to shape. Before I degassed it and began working it, however, I got some coals lit. Then I came in and shaped the dough into four equal quarters and made them into boule shapes (balls). I put these in a square configuration on a piece of parchment on a plate. I could have also done it as a single boule and let it proof on a plate, in a bowl, or in one of my proofing baskets.

Soon the coals were hot, and I put an oiled Dutch oven on and under a lot of coals, probably a total of about 30, with an oven thermometer inside. After about 20 minutes, it read 350 degrees. At this point the dough had proofed up nicely. I lifted the doughballs up by the parchment paper and lowered them into the Dutch oven. I closed the lid and marked the time.

After about fifteen minutes, I rotated the oven and the lid, both a quarter turn, so that the oven was positioned differently in relation to the coals (to prevent hot spots on the oven). I also peeked in and inserted a thermometer into the now-cooking bread.

After about another 20 minutes, the thermometer read 200 degrees, and I knew the bread was done. I pulled the Dutch oven off the coals and dropped the quarter loaves onto my cooling racks. This particular day we made split-pea soup, so I used the loaves as bread bowls. It was delicious!

French Bâtard
in a Cast-Iron Oval Roaster

One year for Christmas I received a cast-iron oval roaster. For the purposes of this book, I don't know if an oval roaster is *technically* a Dutch oven, but it *is* cast iron, you *can* put coals on top and below (with a stand), and you *can* (currently) use them in sanctioned Dutch oven cook-offs. So I'm going to call it a Dutch oven.

You can do all kinds of cool things with an oval roaster, as a Dutch oven chef, that you can't do as well with a regular Dutch oven. One is to cook a full rack of ribs. Another is to lay out a big long fish, like a salmon, on a bed of potatoes or rice. I'd love to steam some rice under a few big king crab legs!

But what had me wanting one of these was the opportunity to do French bread the way it's supposed to be done, as a bâtard. See, there are basically three shapes for French bread. The baguette is a long, thin shape, with a lot of crust and not as much crumb. It's great for dipping and for having alongside soups. The boule (or ball) is a round-shaped hearth loaf. That's easy to do with a traditional Dutch oven, since it's round too. Then there's the bâtard. It's somewhere in between the two. It's shorter and fatter than a baguette, but it isn't fully round like a boule. It has more crust area than the boule but not as much as the baguette. It's also what you find labeled as "French bread" in most American supermarkets.

The problem with the Dutch oven is that you can't do a baguette or a bâtard. It's not long enough. But the oval roaster is!

So I finally made a bâtard of French bread, and it turned out *great*! I basically did the same recipe and procedure as I did when I made the boule before, but I did it in the different shape and different oven. The process takes two days, with a preferment dough that rises overnight. This helps develop more flavor.

TOOLS

Day 1: no Dutch oven needed

Day 2: oval roaster

18–20 coals below

24–26 coals above

a Dutch oven trivet, or stand, to raise the roaster up above the coals

The first step, the night before, is to make a *pâte fermentée*, or a preferment. This is basically a bread dough that you let rise overnight and then use as a basis for more bread dough the next day.

INGREDIENTS: PREFERMENT

½ tsp. yeast

1 cup water

2¼ cups bread flour

¾ tsp. salt

I started by mixing the yeast and the water. It doesn't matter as much if the water's hot here, but I'm used to activating the yeast in 110-degree water. Stir the yeast into the water and let it sit for 10–15 minutes.

While waiting, I sifted the flour and salt together in a mixing bowl. Once the yeast was a little frothy, I poured the yeast/water mix onto the flour and stirred it up. I shook a little flour onto my tabletop and kneaded the dough a bit. I went for a while, but I didn't worry about a windowpane because I knew that I'd be kneading it for real the next day.

I sprayed the bowl with oil, set the doughball in, and sprayed it with oil. I covered the bowl with plastic and let it rise for about an hour.

Then it went into the fridge for the overnight ferment.

INGREDIENTS: THE DOUGH

the pâte fermentée from the night before

1 cup water

1 tsp. yeast

2 cups bread flour, plus more for kneading

¾ tsp. salt

sesame seeds

The next day, I pulled the pâte fermentée out pretty early and set it aside to come up in temperature and rise a little more. I let it sit most of the morning.

When I was ready to work it, I got another cup of 110-degree water (or close to it) and activated a little more yeast. I sifted 2 cups of the flour in a mixing bowl and added the salt. Then, I cut the pâte fermentée into a dozen or so small chunks. Finally, I combined the pâte fermentée, the flour mix, and the yeast mix and stirred it up.

Then I turned the dough out onto my floured tabletop and started kneading and flouring in earnest. This time, I really worked it and kept at it until I got a good stretchy windowpane. Once it was well kneaded, I formed it into a boule, stretching and tucking the surface tight, and set it back into the oiled bowl. I oiled the surface of the bread too and covered it all to rise.

It rose up nicely over the course of a couple of hours. When it had doubled in bulk, I went out and lit up a lot of coals. Once the coals were starting,

I put a little flour on the tabletop and dumped out the dough. I squashed and stretched it into a long, narrow shape, about 1½ feet long by 3–4 inches wide. I stretched it into a tight surface and pinched the bottom tight together all along the length. I put that whole dough loaf onto a single piece of parchment paper (to make it easier to move) and set it aside to rise some more.

Then I went back out to my cooking area with my oval roaster. I spritzed some oil all over the inside and set it up on my lid stand trivet. I put 18–20 coals below it, right under the edge, and 24–26 coals above on the lid. I had limited space on the lid, and it didn't have a high lip to keep the ash in, so I could tell things might get tricky. But I had to work with it.

After 15–20 minutes, the roaster was preheated and the dough had risen back up some. I took my razor, my dough, some hot pads, a short-stemmed thermometer, and my son to start the baking. While I carefully lifted the lid, he lowered the dough in on the parchment. Then he sprinkled on some sesame seeds, cut three long slashes in the top of the dough with the razor, and stuck in the thermometer. I set the lid back on and marked the time. I also put a handful of fresh coals into the chimney to start.

After about 15 minutes, I turned the oven a half turn, and the lid as well, just to change the relative positions of the coals to the bread dough. That helps promote more even cooking. Turning the lid without shaking ash into the oven was tricky. (When I do it now, I knock the ash off the coals and sweep it clean first.) I put a few fresh coals at even distances above and below, mainly because they had burned down and it was very cold out. In the summer, or in a lighter breeze, that might not be necessary.

After another 15–20 minutes, the bread was done. I lifted up the lid and the thermometer read 190 degrees. It can go as high as 200, but the lighter white breads can be done at 190. I shook the ashes off the lid and brought the roaster in. I lifted the bread out by the parchment paper and set it onto my cooling rack. It really looked nice! The crust wasn't too hard, and the bottom was nicely browned as well.

My wife said that it was the best bread I'd ever baked. I had some friends come over and share. It was great by itself, and I also loved it with butter and honey!

Extra note, for a normal Dutch oven:

If you don't happen to have an oval roaster, you can use a regular 12-inch shallow Dutch oven. Shape the dough into a boule instead of a bâtard and use 12 coals below and 20–24 above. Other than that, the procedure is the same. It will still taste amazing, but it will be shaped differently. Make sure that it's cooked all the way through since it's thicker.

Italian Ciabatta

This is a "rustic" bread. The dough is wet and loose. It's also one of those kinds of breads that people call "artisan" breads. I think that's just for good snob appeal. Still, I love trying new things, so I have baked it a few times.

This bread is kind of interesting. It's a wet dough and it has a long pre-ferment time. In fact, it was tricky for me to figure out exactly when to set it up and when to start so that the times of activity (mixing, kneading, baking) and the times of inactivity (rising, proofing, and so on) would all coincide with times that I'd be able to do them.

The wetness of the dough and the extra heat make the crust crispy and make large air bubbles in the crumb. The long fermentation gives it a wonderful flavor.

TOOLS

12-inch Dutch oven

12–14 coals below

24–26 coals above

INGREDIENTS: THE STARTER

⅔ cup water, about 100 degrees

3 Tbsp. milk

½ tsp. dry yeast

¼ tsp. honey

1 cup bread flour

INGREDIENTS: THE DOUGH

½ tsp. dry yeast

1 cup water, about 100 degrees

½ Tbsp. olive oil

2–2½ cups bread flour

1½ tsp. salt

I started early one morning when I got up and made the starter. So many different books call this step so many different things. Some call it the preferment. Others call it the start or the starter. I've heard it called the sponge. At any rate, I combined the water and the milk in a bowl and then dissolved the yeast into that mixture, letting it sit for 5–10 minutes. Then I added the honey. Finally, I stirred in the flour. The mixture was fairly runny and sticky. I set the bowl aside on my kitchen counter, covered by a cloth towel.

About 12 hours later, I looked at the starter. It had foamed up and sank back down. At that point, it was time to make the dough. I added the yeast and the water to activate and dissolve the yeast. I set it aside for 5–10 minutes. I added this mixture and the olive oil to the starter bowl with the starter and mixed that up. It wasn't easy to mix with a wooden spoon.

Next I added 2 cups of flour and kept stirring. The dough should remain sticky and quite loose, not like a good, firm, kneadable dough. I could see that the stirring-up time was the only kneading it was gonna get. Stirring it all over and over for 6–7 minutes was difficult, and tiring to the ol' wrist. I had to do it, though, so I did.

I pulled the dough out of the bowl for a moment and lined the inside of the bowl with parchment paper. Then I put the dough back in. I set the bowl aside with a towel over it, and I let the dough rise for 2½–3 hours.

At 2–2½ hours rising time, I started some coals. I checked the dough, of course, and it had risen a lot! The recipe said to let it rise to triple it's original size, and it had certainly done that. This size helps the dough to have the air bubbles that will expand with the blast of heat.

I lit up my coals, and preheated the oven for 15–20 minutes. With the oven good and hot, I lifted the dough by the parchment and lowered it into the oven. The idea is to handle it as little as possible, so as to avoid degassing it. I sprinkled a little flour on top, mostly for decoration. Then I put the Dutch oven on the coals, with the lid on, and let it bake. I rotated the oven and the lid a quarter turn every 10–15 minutes and replenished the coals as needed.

When the thermometer read done, at 190 degrees, I pulled it out and let it cool. Ciabatta is a great accompaniment to pasta dishes and is great as a dipping bread appetizer.

Rye Bread
Or, My Dog Ate My Homework

One week, I found a cool recipe for a rye bread. I've always liked rye, ever since I was a kid. I've got some fun and fond memories of making sandwiches out of Mom's rye bread. I'd make a killer braunschweiger and Swiss cheese sandwich. My wife, however, hates it. I understand—it does some nasty things to my breath. Still, it tastes great!

My mom also used to make these rye breadsticks and my dad would slice them up at an angle and spread them out on a cookie sheet. He'd set them aside for a couple of days, and they'd get rock hard. He'd slap some cheese on them, and we could hear him crunching them all through the house.

Anyway, I found some rye flour and a good recipe, and I tried it. I got it all baked up, and it was smellin' great. I set it aside to go to church. When I got home, we found that the dog had gotten up on the kitchen counter and eaten the entire loaf.

It's a good thing he's so dang cute. . . . That's pretty much all that saved him.

Anyway, here's the recipe.

TOOLS

12-inch Dutch oven

8–9 coals below

18–19 coals above

INGREDIENTS

2 cups hot water

1½ cups rye flour

¼ cup molasses

¼ cup brown sugar

2 envelopes dry yeast (or 4½ teaspoons yeast)

1 Tbsp. caraway seed

3 Tbsp. oil

1 Tbsp. salt

4 cups white bread flour

This recipe is interesting in that there are three risings/fermentations. First of all, I started by making a "sponge." This is a nasty gloppy goo that sometimes people use to start breads, especially sourdoughs. I mixed all of the first set of ingredients in a big bowl. Then I set that aside to rise for 45–60 minutes.

Then I mixed the second set of ingredients into the first, creating a dough. I started with only 3 cups of flour, though, and then added about a half cup at a time. As I began kneading the dough, it was sticky, so I had to keep adding lots of flour to the tabletop. It kneaded out nicely, once it wasn't so sticky. You never know exactly how much flour you'll need to make it all feel nice and smooth, so don't simply dump in all the flour. It's better to "sneak up on it."

Once the dough was kneaded, I spray-oiled the mixing bowl, and set the dough in to rise, also spraying oil over the dough. The dough rose well, though I don't remember if it was an hour or an hour and a half.

Once the dough had doubled in bulk, I dumped it out of the bowl, punched it down, and formed it into a ball. I put that in the oiled Dutch oven (I used a deep Dutch oven for this recipe). I let it rise for about another hour. During this time, I lit the coals, and when they were getting white, I put a lot of them on the lid of the Dutch oven and set the lid aside to preheat.

Finally, after the lid had preheated, I set the Dutch oven on the coals. The bread baked for 45–60 minutes. This bread was truly magnificent when I took it out to cool. I didn't eat any right away, since we were going to some friends' for dinner, and I had planned on taking it along. No such luck. As a result of my dog, I didn't even taste a slice.

My dog ate pretty well that day. I guess "a dog's life" isn't always so bad, eh?

I didn't kill him, and I made the bread again in a few days. It was as delicious as it looked.

Indian Naan
with Pseudo-Indian Chicken

One night, I made this amazing sort of nouveau/fusion tandoori chicken, and I was wondering what to make to accompany it. I quickly decided that I would try to make naan! Whenever we go out to Indian, we always have it spread with melted garlic butter.

One problem was that when I was making the naan, I saw that the measurement for the flour was in weight. Unfortunately, I don't have a scale, so I simply mixed the flour in until it felt nice and smooth and right.

So, the recipes will reflect the way I actually did it, not so much what the original said. That's typically how I cook anyway! If you're wanting to make only the naan, then ignore all the parts about the chicken, the recipe of which I've included for your enjoyment. But they really do go well together.

THE PSEUDO-INDIAN CHICKEN

TOOLS

12-inch Dutch oven

10–12 coals below

20–24 (or more) coals above (depending on the outside temperature)

INGREDIENTS

2–3 lbs. chicken (I used frozen chicken breast)

1 cup yogurt

4 Tbsp. garam masala powder

salt

oil

THE GARLIC NAAN

TOOLS

12-inch Dutch oven

10–12 coals below

20–24 (or more) coals above (depending on the outside temperature)

INGREDIENTS

2 tsp. dry active yeast

4 Tbsp. warm milk

2 tsp. sugar

2–3 cups flour

1 tsp. baking powder

½ tsp. salt

⅔ cup milk

⅔ cup yogurt

1 egg

2 Tbsp. butter

½ stick butter, softened

2 Tbsp. minced garlic

liberal shakes of parsley and thyme

salt and pepper to taste

Since I cooked these things at the same time, I'll go over the instructions as I did them. There's a few suggestions I'll throw in that I hope to remember to do next time.

I patted the thawed chicken dry and cut a few slices into the chicken so the spices could more easily penetrate. I put it in a bowl with the yogurt, the garam masala powder, the salt, and the oil and stirred it up. I set this aside for a couple of hours.

Then, I mixed the first set of ingredients in the naan section to activate the yeast. I let it sit until it got frothy and then added the next set of ingredients. I mixed it all together (a little shy on the flour), then turned it out onto the floured tabletop to knead. As I kneaded it, I added more flour bit by bit until it felt right, smooth and satiny. Then I set the dough aside to rise.

When I came back a couple of hours later, the chicken and the bread were both almost ready.

I lit up a lot of coals. (Hey, it was cold out!) The tandoori chicken is normally cooked in a special oven that cooks with a very dry heat so the marinade gets baked onto the chicken dry. Dutch ovens, of course, trap the steam and hot moisture under a heavy cast-iron lid. Also, if you just put the chicken in the bottom of the oven, the juices will gather around the chicken. My solution was to put the chicken in one of those folding steamers (so the juices would drip down below) and put that into the Dutch oven. I dealt with the lid another way (see method below). I put that oven on the coals to begin cooking.

I oiled the other 12-inch Dutch oven up and put it on and under the coals to preheat.

Then, I cut the dough into quarters and rolled and spread each quarter until flat on the floured tabletop. I had mixed the butter and the spices, so I spread that over each flat. I put one flat into the Dutch oven and set on the lid. After 3–5 minutes, I opened up the lid and turned the bread over to cook for another 3–5 minutes. Then I pulled it out and put in the next one.

In the meantime, the chicken was cooking. I put some more of the sauce/marinade on after a bit. After about 20 minutes on the heat, I figured the chicken was about half done. I had this set of tongs that I balanced across the rim of the Dutch oven and put the lid back on it. That lifted the lid enough to let the steam vent, but not so much that too much heat was lost as well. Another idea I had was to get a few 2-inch nails, at least 3 of them, and to bend them into a U-shape. Place them over the side of the Dutch oven so when the lid is put back on, it sits high. I put a lot of extra coals on the lid so there was extra heat radiating from the top as well.

After about another 20 minutes, the chicken was done and ready.

Italian Focaccia
in a Cast-Iron Oval Roaster

Bringing this bread to pass was quite a fight. First of all, this is an "indirect" bread, meaning it requires a preferment rise before the regular rise. That means the recipe is at least a two-day project to do it right.

Then, after the preferment, it takes another four hours of mixing, kneading, rising, and baking. It's a long process.

On a Saturday night, I made the "poolish," which is a wet, gloppy goo, and let it rise overnight in the fridge. On Sunday, when I went to work on it, I mixed the full dough (which is still quite wet), and while it was rising, my dogs got to it and made off with over half the dough. I was *not* happy.

It wasn't until the following Friday and Saturday that I would have the proper time available for the whole process. Fortunately, this time it worked.

Focaccia is a flat rustic bread. It comes from a wet dough, and it is flat and often carries toppings. I wondered, as I was making it, if it was a forerunner of pizza, or maybe a descendant.

When I baked this, I did it in the oval roaster. If you do it in regular Dutch ovens, I would recommend doing it in two twelve-inch ovens, with twelve coals below and twenty-two to twenty-four coals above.

TOOLS

oval roaster

25 coals below

35 coals above

INGREDIENTS: THE POOLISH

2½ cups unbleached bread flour

1½ cups warm water

½ tsp. yeast

INGREDIENTS: THE BREAD

¾ cup warm water

1½ tsp. yeast

2½ cups unbleached bread flour, plus more for working dough

2 tsp. salt

6 Tbsp. olive oil

3 cups poolish

INGREDIENTS: THE HERBAL OIL

2 cups olive oil, warmed

½ cup dried mixed herbs

parsley

oregano

sage

rosemary

any other herbs

1 Tbsp. salt

½ Tbsp. ground black pepper

INGREDIENTS: THE TOPPINGS

any toppings you want—I used:

½ medium onion, diced

2–3 cloves garlic, diced

1 Roma tomato, diced

4–6 oz. of a blend of italian cheeses: mozzarella,
   Asiago, Parmesan

I started mixing the poolish the night before baking. Of all the processes, this first step was probably the easiest. I simply mixed the three ingredients thoroughly and then covered it in plastic and set it aside for 1–2 hours. It rose up nicely. I put it in the fridge to continue the fermentation overnight. Longer ferment times make for more rich flavors!

The next day, I took the poolish out of the fridge early. The poolish was a bit bigger, but not by much. I let it sit for an hour or so to warm up a bit. After a while, I measured out the 110-degree water and sprinkled in the yeast, to activate it.

Then, I got a large ceramic mixing bowl, sifted in the flour, and added the salt. I added in all of the wet ingredients: the yeast/water mix, the olive oil, and the poolish. (The poolish was quite gluteny, even though it was runny, so it was difficult to measure. I ended up spooning it into a measuring cup.) I started mixing with a heavy wooden spoon.

. . . But then it got ugly.

I stuck my hand in the goo and started squeezing it through my fingers, turning the bowl as I went. I would squeeze, turn, release, then grab another glob and squeeze again. It felt *sooo* gross. This was taking the place of a normal knead. As I was doing this, I could feel it getting more smooth and gluteny. I did that for almost 8 minutes. This process was quite tiring on the fingers. Finally, I rubbed what I could off my fingers and then rinsed my hands. It really was a mess.

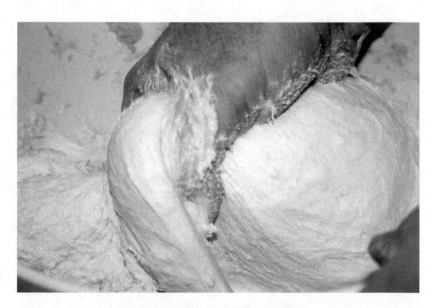

Then I sprinkled a small handful of flour out onto the countertop, in about the size and shape of a dinner plate. I dumped the goo dough onto it (scraping the sides of the bowl with a spatula), and sprinkled more flour on top. I floured my hands and grabbed each side and pulled, stretching the dough outward.

I folded the right side over the middle and then the left side to form a small square, which I gently flattened a bit.

I turned the dough 90 degrees and did the stretch and folds again. Then I covered it with a tea towel and let it sit for 30 minutes.

I mixed the herbal oil next: I put the olive oil in a jar and then set the jar in some really hot water for a time. I added in all of the herbs and seasonings for the herbal oil and stirred it up. The heat makes the oil absorb the flavors a bit more.

After the 30-minute rest, I did the stretch and fold again, and after that, I did another 30-minute rise/rest. Finally, after one more stretch and fold, it was ready for shaping.

I got a lot of coals lit. I was shooting for a final temperature of 450 degrees.

I poured a liberal amount of the herbal oil in the bottom of the oval roaster, enough to lightly cover the bottom. I put in the dough and, using my fingertips, stretched it out to the edges, or at least close to it. I pressed my fingertips into the dough, all the way to the pot, to make the traditional dimples.

I poured on more herbal oil and then sprinkled on the onions, garlic, and tomatoes. Then I let that rise some more. I also put in a short-stemmed thermometer.

In a pizza, the crust gives a delicious carriage for the toppings. In focaccia, the bread is the attention, and the toppings should simply enhance it. The first time I made this (as shown in the final picture), I went overboard on the toppings. It still tasted great, but there wasn't a real edgy crust, and the toppings kept the dough quite moist in spots.

When the coals were white-edged, I took the lid out and put as many coals on it as I could. I wanted it heck-hot! Another 15 minutes and the dough was ready, the lid was ready, and it was time to bake.

I put the lid on and set the roaster on the stand, to lift it up above the coals. I used the proper amount of coals above and below and let it bake.

After about 15 minutes, I lifted the lid and saw that the dough was cooking nicely. I added the cheese at that point. I actually put on a lot of cheese. In retrospect, I would put on less than half what I did, and I might even wait another five minutes. Removing 6–8 coals from the middle of the top would have probably been a good idea at this point as well.

After another 10 minutes, the thermometer registered 200 degrees, so I shook off the coals, and, using a pancake turner, I tipped the roaster and lifted the focaccia out, laying it nicely onto a cooling rack. It sat there, teasing me, for about 1 hour.

In spite of the darkened top, the whole bread tasted amazing. The herb oil and the oil in the dough gave it a richness, and the toppings were delicious. It didn't have the big holes in the crumb that I had hoped for, but the crumb was deliciously light and flavorful.

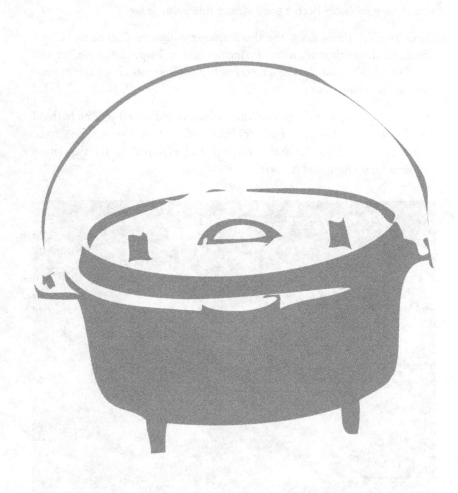

Chapter 6
Topped, Stuffed, and Filled Breads

ONE OF the big reasons we have bread is, of course, to eat it. But one of the biggest reasons we now make bread is to eat it with something else in it or on it. I mean, really, how often do most folks eat bread straight from the bag when they bring it home. Okay, I do sometimes. Still, most of the bread that you get sliced from the grocery store is fairly empty of flavor or body. Not much point in eating it without something to add on.

Sandwiches are only a part of the game. We make so many breads and doughs fully intending from the start to put stuff on top, to fill with stuff, or to wrap stuff inside.

One of my favorites is, of course, pizza. So much so that Dutch oven pizza was the first thing I made when my wife bought me that first Dutch oven, lo, these many years ago.

Pizza

The secret to good pizza is easy. That secret demonstrates an important principle I've been learning about cooking, especially with the Dutch oven. That principle is GIGO.

Those of you who are into computers, especially programming, already understand this term. It means "garbage in, garbage out." In this case, in the culinary world, I'm referring to ingredients: if you make a dish with garbage, it's going to taste like garbage. The opposite is also true. If you use good stuff to make your food, it will taste great. So to make good pizza, don't scrimp on your ingredients. A good dough recipe, good sauce, and good toppings make great pizza.

I must confess, though, that the first time I did pizza, I used a crust mix from a box. To do that now, I would hang my head in shame. It turned out fairly well, considering. The second time I made pizza, I found an actual rising bread recipe and did it instead. Over time, I've refined the process. Here's how to do it right:

TOOLS

12-inch Dutch oven

20+ coals below, for the sausage

10–12 coals below, for the baking

20–22 coals above

INGREDIENTS: THE CRUST

1 Tbsp. yeast

1½ cups warm water

1 Tbsp. sugar

3 Tbsp. oil

4 cups flour

¼ tsp. salt

INGREDIENTS: THE SAUCE

1 (6-oz.) can tomato paste

1 (8-oz.) can tomato sauce

liberal shakes of:

oregano

basil

rosemary

garlic powder

salt

pepper

INGREDIENTS: THE PAN COATING

garlic powder or garlic salt

any other flavorings you'd like (salt, pepper, paprika, and so on)

INGREDIENTS: TOPPINGS

½ lb. mild Italian sausage

8–16 oz. shredded mozzarella

sliced pepperoni

canadian bacon/ham slices or cubes

diced onions

diced green peppers

minced olives

First, I dissolved the yeast in the warm water. Then I added the sugar, a little at a time. After it got all foamy, I added and the oil, beating for a few minutes. I added 2 cups of flour and the salt. I mixed it, adding the rest of the flour gradually to make a soft dough. I kneaded it for 10–15 minutes or so, adding flour to adjust for the moisture, until I could get a good windowpane. Then I set it aside to rise for about 45 minutes or so and then put it in the fridge.

When it was time to start making the pizza (or even about an hour before) I pulled the dough out of the fridge and let it warm up a bit and even rise a little more. Next I mixed up the sauce ingredients, tasting it to make sure that the flavors were even. Then I fired up the coals.

In a 12-inch Dutch oven, I cooked the sausage. (I like Italian sausage, as opposed to the common breakfast pork sausage. Still the breakfast stuff is good too.) I spread the grease around the bottom and sides as I stirred the sausage bits.

When the sausage was browned, I pulled the oven off the coals, pulled the sausage out, and sprinkled some garlic powder or garlic salt, as well as any other pan coating flavorings, across the bottom of the Dutch oven. This makes for a great flavoring in the crust.

Then I stretched out the dough and spread it evenly on the bottom of the oven with my fingers. I like it pretty thick, so it was more of a deep-dish pizza. If you like thinner crust, you can chop the dough in half and use 2 Dutch ovens.

I spread on the sauce with the back of a spoon. (You can lay it on thick or thin, as you like it.) Then I sprinkled on a little bit of grated mozzarella and started layering on the other toppings. Here's where the real critical make-or-break stuff happens. Get good, fresh toppings and be liberal with them. Put on the sausage, the pepperoni (and please, more than one pepperoni per slice), the fresh onions, the olives, and so on. Go for it and lay out what you like.

Finally I smothered (and yes, I mean smothered) it all in a deep blanket of more mozzarella.

I put the oven back on the coals and baked it for about 30 minutes. When the top cheese was melty and brown and I could see the crust was done, I pulled the Dutch oven off the coals.

I cut it with a plastic knife and served it right from the Dutch. This pizza is incredible, and since there are so many toppings, it's very filling.

Chicago-Style Pizza

If regular-style pizza is somehow not extreme enough for you . . .

On our recent trip to Indiana, we stopped over for a night with our friend in Chicago, and she treated us to a Chicago-style pizza dinner. It's bigger and heftier than most pizzas, with a sauced-up crust on top and on the bottom. Oh, it was *sooooo* good and so filling. I loved it, and I knew instantly that I had to try doing it in the Dutch oven. It took me a while to get around to it, but here it is.

I got a book during the trip about Chicago-style pizzas, and I followed the crust recipe fairly closely, but I experimented with the toppings and some other things a bit. I doubled the crust recipe and made two different pies, each with unique fillings. I liked both of the ones I did.

I was also concerned with the cooking time because the pizza was so much thicker than pizzas I'd cooked before. The parbaking and the adjusted cook time made a big difference.

TOOLS

2 (12-inch) Dutch ovens

10–12 coals below

18–22 coals above

INGREDIENTS: THE CRUST

3 tsp. sugar

2 Tbsp. active dry yeast

1¼ cups warm water

4 cups bread flour

3 tsp. salt

3 Tbsp. dough enhancer

4 Tbsp. olive oil

INGREDIENTS: THE FILLINGS

4 oz. shredded mozzarella

The following are optional (but the more fillings, the merrier):

½ lb. mild or medium Italian sausage

cubed ham

pepperoni slices

onions, diced

green peppers, diced

Roma tomatoes, diced

baby spinach leaves, julienned

black olives, chopped

fresh mushrooms

anything else you like

INGREDIENTS: THE PAN COATING

garlic powder

salt

olive oil

INGREDIENTS: THE SAUCE

1 (6-oz.) can tomato paste

1 (8-oz.) can tomato sauce

2 fresh Roma tomatoes, diced

3–4 cloves garlic, minced

liberal shakes of:

oregano

basil

rosemary

salt

pepper

4 oz. shredded mozzarella

I made the dough essentially like every other bread dough I've done. I mixed the sugar, the yeast, and the water. I did that a little more carefully this time, however, because I wanted to keep it at 110–115 degrees. So, I poured in the hot/warm water a bit at a time and monitored the temperature as the sugar dissolved, adding hotter water to keep it "in the zone." It rewarded me by foaming up quite nicely.

I sifted the dry ingredients, starting with just 3 cups of flour. The rest I would add during kneading.

Then I mixed in the olive oil and kneaded the dough on the tabletop, adding flour onto it as needed to make it not so sticky (yet still soft). I set the dough aside to rise, but since I was going to be doing other stuff for a long time that day, I set it in the fridge.

When I came home, I pulled the dough out of the fridge first. It had risen up nicely. I punched it down and cut it into halves, which I formed into small boules. I set these aside to proof and come up to room temperature.

Then I started up the coals, and as soon as they were ready, I put the Dutch oven on 20 or more coals. I put the sausage in and browned it, separating it into small chunks as I went. While I was doing that, I was also chopping up the onions, peppers, and other fillings. I got some more coals started as well, and I put 20 or so hot coals on each lid to begin preheating.

Once the sausage was browned, I scooped it out. I added a little bit of garlic powder, salt, and olive oil to the Dutch oven and spread that around the bottom. That and the sausage flavoring would give the crust a great taste! I stretched out some dough, pretty evenly, and spread enough to cover the bottom of the Dutch oven. You should have one remaining doughball to set aside. I tried to press the dough in the Dutch oven up the sides as much as possible. I took a fork and poked holes in the crust every inch or so.

Then I parbaked the crust, or, in other words, I baked it a bit before I added the fillings and bake it for real. At the time I wasn't sure why you would do that, but later I realized that there is going to be a lot of food on the crust. It will be thick and heavy. In order for that bottom crust to stand up, it needs to have some poof and structure first.

So after the crust was spread, I put the heated lid on and put about 8 coals below and 18 coals above the Dutch oven. I let it bake for only a few minutes—I recommend checking it after 12–15 minutes. The crust should be a bit firm but not browned. While that was baking, I made the sauce. The sauce was easy: I mixed everything except the mozzarella and blended it to taste in a bowl.

Then I took the Dutch oven off the heat, opened it up, and put the fillings of choice on the crust. I started with a layer of the mozzarella and then added everything else. I did two pizzas, so I tried slightly different combinations of toppings. I did cubed ham, pepperoni, and the sausage I'd cooked. I actually quartered the pepperoni slices too, to make them more like chunks. In one Dutch oven, I added onions and peppers, and in the other I put the spinach and the tomatoes. I kept the fillings away from the edge of the crust.

Then I stretched out the remaining dough and laid it on top. I reached under the edge of the pizza and pinched the two crusts together, sealing all around the circle. I pressed on the top to kind of spread it back out to the edge of the Dutch oven.

Once the Dutch oven was ready, I put it on and under the coals and let it bake, turning it from time to time. I baked it for 15–20 minutes. Then, I checked it. It was getting done and starting to brown on top nicely, so I spread the sauce and the cheese over the top and baked it for another 20–30 minutes.

In the end, it tasted great! One slice is a full meal. Have two if you're either famished or foolhardy!

Mark's Own Calzone

For a long time, before I'd even tried the Chicago-style pizza above, I'd wanted to try a pizza with a crust on the bottom and on the top. So, one day, I thought I'd try calzones. The process ended up being a pretty involved two-day affair because I decided I wanted to try an overnight rise on the crust.

THE CRUST

INGREDIENTS

1 Tbsp. yeast

1½ cups hot water

1 Tbsp. sugar

¼ tsp. salt

3 Tbsp. oil

4 cups bread flour

THE FILLING/SAUCE

TOOLS

10-inch Dutch oven

15–18 coals below

INGREDIENTS

½ lb. mild italian sausage

¼ lb. bacon, cut into short strips

1 link of pepperoni, quartered and chopped

1 full Tbsp. flour

½ medium onion, diced

2–3 cloves garlic, minced

2 stalks celery, chopped

1 green pepper, chopped

½ jalapeño; seeded, cored, and chopped

6–7 Roma tomatoes, diced

about ½ cup water

THE CALZONES

TOOLS

12-inch Dutch oven

10–12 coals below

16–18 coals above

INGREDIENTS

1 egg, beaten

about 2 cups shredded mozzarella

fresh chopped Italian parsley

freshly grated Parmesan and/or myzithra cheeses

The process started the night before. At the time, I had read a lot about how the longer overnight rises are better for pizza, and I thought I'd try it that way. Spoiler alert: I'm definitely sold on that now. Years later, I don't do it any other way.

I proofed the yeast in water that was hot, but not scalding, to the touch. I say it's "shower" hot. That's 110–115 degrees, and it's great for waking up yeast. While that was getting foamy and frothy, I added the other crust ingredients to a bowl. Then I added the yeast/water mix.

I stirred the mixture up and found that it was just the right hydration, this time. I say, "this time" because different flours and different humidities can mean that the flour will absorb more or less water. You just never know. I started kneading it on the countertop, and I found I didn't need to add any more flour in the process.

I set the dough in a greased bowl, covered it with cellophane, and placed it in the fridge. I knew I wasn't going to use it until the next day, and I wanted it to have a long, slow, flavor-developing rise overnight in the fridge.

Then I went and played cards with some friends.

The next day, I pulled the bread dough out of the fridge and set it aside in the kitchen to come up to room temperature. I also lit up some coals, and put the lightly oiled 10-inch Dutch oven on some coals to season and heat up. Once it was smoking a little bit, I put in the sausage, the bacon, and the pepperoni pieces. I used link pepperoni cut into small chunks, but you could use sliced pepperoni. I'd still probably cut the slices in half or into wedges. The sausage cooked, the bacon crisped, and the pepperoni browned.

Once the meat was done, I pulled it out but left the drippings. I sprinkled in the flour and stirred while it cooked into a roux. I scooped it out as best I could and then tossed in the onion, garlic, celery, green pepper, and jalapeño to sweat and sauté. I kept the oven hot all along the way with fresh coals.

Finally, I added the tomatoes and the water and then brought the meat and the roux back in as well. I let it boil at first, and then simmer, covered, to give the tomatoes time to dissolve as much as possible. I let it go maybe as much as 1 hour. The mixture should be nice and "sauce" thick. If it's still runny at that point, let it cook a bit longer with the lid off.

I was tasting it all along the way. With all of the sausages and bacon, it didn't need much salt, if any, and probably didn't need many other seasonings. Once the sauce was done simmering, I poured it out of the Dutch oven into a bowl right away so the tomatoes wouldn't eat away at the patina.

I dumped the bread out onto my floured countertop and cut it into quarters. Then, I stretched each piece out into a wide and thin circle. I put a generous amount of sauce/filling over one half of the dough circle. I left at least a half inch or so to the edge of the dough. I put a generous amount of shredded mozzarella on top of the mound of filling. I brushed some freshly beaten egg onto that edge of the dough, as a sealer. I folded the dough over, and began pinching and curling the dough halves together. Finally, I gently lifted the finished calzone into the oiled 12-inch Dutch oven.

I followed the same process for the other calzones. Hopefully, there should be a good amount of sauce leftover for all of them. Then, I brushed all the calzones with the beaten egg, giving a good coating. I let that Dutch oven sit to let the dough continue rising a bit.

In the meantime, I'd been starting up some additional coals, and I put those on the 12-inch lid to heat it up. After the lid was really hot and the dough had proofed a little bit, I set a ring of coals below the Dutch oven and set the lid with the coals on top. I watched and maintained the heat with fresh coals as needed.

I took the bread temperature by sticking a thermometer down in between the calzones, where the crusts grew together. (Taking the temperature of the filling was kinda pointless since it was all completely cooked already.) I let it get a little bit overly done because I wasn't sure how it would react to the filling. That turned out to be a good thing. It was perfect.

I cut the calzones apart and served them with more sauce drizzled over the top, with a garnish of chopped parsley and grated cheese.

The calzones were big and filling, and they had an incredible taste!

Chapter 7
Creative Bread Recipes

THROUGHOUT MY years of breadmaking trial and error, trying to unlock the secrets of the yeast and the grain, I hit on a few combinations that were more like trial and success! After a few years, those started happening with greater and greater frequency, until I learned that I could come up with some original ideas and make them work fairly consistently.

Let me share with you some of the originals that have come out of my kitchen and blog!

Swirled Bread

At one point in my Dutch oven breadmaking career, I wanted to mix up a light white bread and a darker bread and then combine them. I wasn't quite sure how I wanted to combine them, but I had a couple of ideas. One was to create two flat panels of each dough, stack them, and roll them, kinda like a cinnamon roll. The other was to create a couple of long ropes, twist them over and around each other, and then wrap that in a circle in the Dutch oven.

In the end, I found that I like the "cinnamon roll" idea the best. Consistently, it gives the most visually stunning results.

TOOLS

12-inch Dutch oven

10–12 coals below

20–22 coals above

INGREDIENTS

1 cup hot water

½ cup honey

1 Tbsp. yeast

½ tsp. salt

1 egg

1 cup milk

¼ cup oil

4–5 cups flour

1 heaping Tbsp. cocoa

1 heaping Tbsp. coffee substitute (I used Pero)

2 Tbsp. molasses

1–2 cups flour, for the kneading

1 egg, beaten

I started with the hot water and the honey. Yeast activates best in water that's at about 110 degrees. Use even hotter water here because when you add the honey, the water will cool considerably. Then I added the yeast and let that sit to foam up while I gathered the other ingredients.

I mixed everything in the second set of ingredients into the bowl with the first set and stirred it all up with the ol' wooden spoon. When I'm mixing at this stage, I tend to go with less flour, and I tend to add more in the kneading process.

With it all stirred up into a gloppy goo, I separated them into two equal batches. Into one batch, which would be the dark swirl, I added all of the ingredients from the third set. Then I kneaded each batch separately, adding more flour as I went to keep it from sticking, and kneaded until each batch passed the windowpane test. Then I set each one aside to rise.

In 1–1½ hours, they were ready. The dark one rose more, I think because of the extra sugar in the molasses.

Once they'd risen, I rolled each one out flat and shaped them into squares. I put one on top of the other, like stacking paper. I rolled them up and then kind of mushed the ends toward the middle so it was a little more ball shaped. I put that into the oiled Dutch oven to proof.

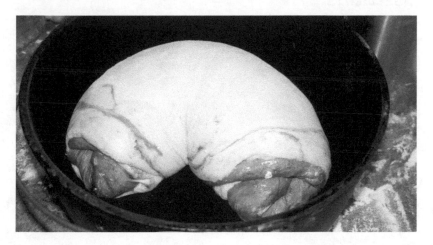

While this was proofing, I lit up some coals. Once the coals were lit, I put 20–25 coals on top of the lid to preheat it.

By the time the lid was heated, the bread was nicely risen in the Dutch oven. I coated the loaf in the beaten egg to give it a nice sheen on top. Then I made a ring of coals and put the Dutch oven on, with the lid on the oven. From there, I replenished the coals as necessary and turned the lid and the oven every 15 minutes or so. I baked it to an internal temperature of 190–200 degrees.

Then I took off the lid and brought the Dutch oven inside to cool and let the bread cool with it. We served it up with the dinner my wife's cousin brought over. Yummy!

The hardest part is waiting to cut it while it cools! The look of that slice of bread with the swirl of dark in it is priceless. It looks good, and it tastes rich!

Cocoa Bread

This bread was a lot of fun, and it was a total surprise. I started out making one of my ordinary sandwich breads. But then, I took a step to the side!

TOOLS

12-inch Dutch oven

10–12 coals below

20–22 coals above

INGREDIENTS

1 Tbsp. yeast

1 cup hot water (110 degrees)

2 Tbsp. sugar

½ tsp. salt

1 egg

1 cup milk

4–5 cups flour

2 heaping Tbsp. cocoa

I started by proofing the yeast in the water and sugar. I let it sit aside to get all frothy and foamy. Then I mixed in all of the remaining ingredients except cocoa. As usual, I held back a cup or so of flour to add in during the mixing.

As I was mixing ingredients, I got a wild streak, and I added cocoa powder. Why not? The cool thing about bread is that once you get consistent results from a basic core recipe, you can add any kind of enrichments. Flavorings, herbs, fruits, nuts, seeds . . . anything you like.

I kneaded the dough, and even though it took a while to get to the right amount of flour in the mix, it windowpaned nicely.

Anyway, I set it aside to rise, and when I came back about 1½ hours later, it looked incredible. So nicely risen, with a smooth texture. Mmmmm. . . . It looked like a whole wheat-recipe, even though it was made with white flour. I punched the dough down reshaped it into a boule. I spread a towel over a bowl and put the dough in the bowl, on top of the towel, to proof.

I started some coals and preheated the Dutch oven with coals above and below. I made a bottom ring of 12 coals and then about 24 on top. Now, keep in mind that I made this bread in the dead of winter, but there wasn't much wind. It was probably about 30 degrees out that morning. You can adjust your coals according to your circumstances. When the Dutch oven was heated, I opened it up and turned the dough out of the towel into the Dutch oven. I sliced the top of the bread and closed up the lid, marking the time.

I rotated the Dutch oven and the lid every 15–20 minutes. After about 25 minutes, I put the thermometer in. I took the Dutch oven off the coals a little early too—at about 180 degrees. I brought the hot oven inside and left the bread in. After about 10 minutes, the bread was up to an internal temperature of 190, and I took it out of the oven to fully cool.

It was then that I saw how soft the lower crust was and how nice the texture and thickness of the upper crust was as well. I was a little nervous that the crumb would still be doughy, but there hadn't been crumbs sticking to the thermometer when I pulled it out.

Once the bread cooled, I cut into it, and it was deliciously cooked through all the way. When you do something and it all works, and the magic comes together, it's a good feeling.

Hot Bread with Red Pepper and Garlic

When I made this recipe, I hadn't made bread in a long time. By the time I tried this one, I was itching to get my fingers in the dough. I wanted the bread to be different too. I looked through some of my bread books for a bread I hadn't tried yet, but most of the really cool ones were two-day recipes, so I abandoned that. I found a cool recipe online at The Fresh Loaf, but, as usual, I tweaked it.

. . . What? What?

I do that.

And to make matters worse, I decided on some flavorful enrichments, like crushed red pepper and minced garlic.

The result was wonderful!

TOOLS

12-inch shallow Dutch oven

12 coals below

24–26 coals above

INGREDIENTS

3 tsp. yeast

1 cup hot water

4–5 cups bread flour, plus more for kneading

2 tsp. salt

1½ Tbsp. dough enhancer (optional, but I like it sometimes)

2 cloves garlic, minced

2 tsp. crushed dried red pepper

2 cups buttermilk

1 Tbsp. honey

1 egg

topping (I used kosher salt)

First, I added the yeast to the 110-degree water and set the mixture aside to proof.

Then I mixed all of the second set of ingredients. I poured in the frothing yeast, followed by the buttermilk and the honey, and mixed it all up. I dumped all of that out onto a floured countertop and started kneading. Most recipes say to knead for 10 minutes. I use the windowpane test, and I find it can take as much as double that, depending on how fresh and good the flour is. Add more flour if the dough is too sticky. If needed, you can add more water to the mix simply by getting your hands wet and kneading more. I had to do that this time.

Once the dough was kneaded, I set it aside in an oiled bowl, covered, to rise. I let it rise until it was doubled in bulk. For me, with this recipe, that meant about 2 hours.

When the rising was almost done, I started the coals. As soon as a lot of the coals were getting white, I set about 25 coals on the Dutch oven lid. I let the lid preheat like that.

Meanwhile, I did a quick oil spray of the inside of the Dutch oven and put the doughball in it. I beat the egg up and washed it over the top of the dough, and I sprinkled the dough with kosher salt. I sliced the top three times to give it steam vents and to better allow for expansion. I let the dough sit for another 20 minutes or so, to open up a bit, while the lid was preheating.

Then, I put out a ring of 12 coals, set the Dutch oven on it, set the hot lid on top, and marked the time. After 15 minutes, I turned the Dutch oven and the lid and poured some more fresh coals on the pile of spare hot ones. In another fifteen minutes, I turned the oven and lid again and added a few coals to the top and bottom. I also opened up the lid and inserted the thermometer.

After 45 minutes total, the bread was done, with an internal temperature of 190 degrees. The crust was brown and soft, including the under crust. I pulled the bread out and set it on my cooling rack. I gave it quite a while before I sliced it too. Don't cut your bread too soon! It's still cooking while it cools.

The taste was great. The peppers gave it a little bite, and the garlic was more of a subtle addition. You might want to add more per your taste. This bread is great by itself or with meat sandwiches.

Mark's Spice Bread

I saw a recipe for spice bread online several months before I did this, and I'd wanted to do it ever since. I lost the recipe, but I had this general idea for the spices, so I felt like I could try it anyway.

I have to say that this is quite possibly the tastiest bread I've ever made—it almost tastes like a cake. I was really nervous about the spice mix. I tried to sample it beforehand, but it's tough to tell how it'll turn out with the bread and the honey.

TOOLS

12-inch Dutch oven

10 coals below

20 coals above

INGREDIENTS

1 Tbsp. yeast

1 cup hot water

¾ cup honey

2 tsp. spice mix, made of ½ tsp. each of ground cloves, cardamom, cinnamon, paprika, nutmeg, and dried ground ginger

2 Tbsp. olive oil

4–5 cups flour, plus about 1 cup to be added during kneading

a pinch of salt

1 cup milk

1 egg

1 egg, for coating (optional)

I started by activating the yeast in the 110-degree water and honey. I let the mixture sit for quite a while until it became frothy and bubbly. I love the smell of yeast in the morning.

While that was frothing up, I played with the spice mix. I didn't really know what I was getting or anything, I just chose a bunch of spices that I knew or that I had read work well in sweet dishes, like apple pies or banana breads or things like that. I'd also read that oils can extract the flavors of spices, so after I'd mixed the spices up, I put a couple of full teaspoons into the olive oil. I tasted it, but I wasn't sure if it would be enough spice to flavor a whole loaf of bread.

Once the yeast water was bubbly, I added the ingredients in the third set (except optional egg for coating) and the oil/spice mix and stirred it all up. From that point on, it was just a matter of kneading and rising and baking just like any other loaf of bread.

I kneaded the dough, adding more flour until it wasn't sticky. I kneaded it until it got a good stretch on the windowpane test. I knew that I was on the right track because I tasted a little pinch of the dough, and it was *gooooooood*.

I set the dough aside to rise for about 1½ hours. Once that was done, I reshaped it into a boule and set it aside on a cloth to proof.

Then I lit up the coals, and, once they were white, I got them under and over the oiled Dutch oven to preheat. Once it was hot, I used the cloth to carry the dough and flipped it over into the Dutch oven. Then I sliced the top of the dough, set the lid back on the Dutch oven, and marked the time. Optionally, you could also coat the dough with a whipped egg wash.

After 15–20 minutes, I turned the oven and the lid, and I opened it to slip in the thermometer. Another 20 minutes or so and it read well over 190 degrees, ready to come in. I flipped the bread over onto my cooling rack and let it cool.

I admit, the bread was still fairly warm when I finally cut it and tasted it. The spices, and the melting butter I used, made it so good!

GETTING CREATIVE AND MAKING YOUR OWN BREAD RECIPES

By the time you get to this point, you've probably had a bit of practice with some of the recipes included in this book. You might have tried some of your own family bread recipes or some breads you've seen in other cookbooks. You've probably developed some sense of heat management, and you've probably had a few successful baking days!

I hope by now you've also noticed that most of these breads are similar at their core. They include flour, yeast, salt, and water. So, if that's all that lies at the heart of a good loaf of bread, then making variations should really be pretty simple, shouldn't it?

In a previous chapter, I said that once you have the core ingredients, everything else is just an enrichment. So inventing your own recipes is really simply a matter of tossing your own additives into a basic core recipe.

Here's a great basic recipe. It's fairly close to French or Italian bread, and it just adds a little sugar to stimulate yeast growth. It doesn't use the long preferment to develop the natural flour/yeast flavors, so flavors will have to derive from the enrichments and enhancements that you add in.

Core Bread

TOOLS

12-inch Dutch Oven

14–15 coals below

18–22 coals above

INGREDIENTS

1 Tbsp. yeast

2 cups hot water (110 degrees)

2 Tbsp. sugar

1 tsp. salt

about 5 cups fresh bread flour

As you can see, it's very basic. Below, I've listed some suggestions for flavorings and enhancements that you can choose from. They're described in much more detail in chapter three.

OILS: olive oil, vegetable oil, butter, shortening

DAIRY: milk, yogurt, sour cream, cheeses

EGG

SWEETENERS: sugar, brown sugar, honey, molasses, agave nectar

COLORINGS: food coloring, tomato paste, berry syrup/puree, cocoa, coffee substitute, saffron

SEASONINGS AND HERBS

RAISINS, DRIED FRUITS, NUTS

TOPPINGS: egg, butter, milk, cheese, seeds/herbs/seasonings, glazes, flour, cornmeal

Begin with a concept. Start with the core recipe and choose your additives. Finally, choose your toppings. Follow through all the steps in chapter three, and you'll have your own unique, original bread. Give it a name and proudly start a family tradition.

When it's done, ask yourself: Did it not come out quite right? Was one flavor too strong? Was it not what you expected? Try it again and tweak up the ingredients. Change the amounts or add a different flavor. Never give up until you've baked your perfect signature loaf! Then, try something else!

Here I've included some recipes that I created this way.

Tomato Bread

TOOLS

12-inch Dutch oven

14–15 coals below

18–22 coals above

INGREDIENTS

2 Tbsp. olive oil

2 tsp. basil

2 tsp. oregano

1 Tbsp. yeast

2 cups hot water

2 Tbsp. sugar

about 5 cups bread flour

1 tsp. salt

1 (6-oz.) can tomato paste

1 egg

more basil, oregano, and oil for the topping

The first thing I did, about an hour before making the rest of the recipe, was to mix the oil, basil, and oregano in a small bowl. Actually, I used a ramekin. It was the right size, and it was handy. I let the mixture sit so that the flavors of the herbs would release into the oil.

Then, a while later, I mixed the yeast, 110-degree water, and sugar and let that sit for a while to get all frothy and yeasty. While that was proofing, I prepared the other ingredients. I sifted all but one cup of the flour in a bowl and added the salt. Finally, I added the oil/herb mixture, the yeast mixture, the tomato paste, and the egg. Then I stirred it up.

I turned the dough out onto the floured board and started kneading. Right away, I could tell that the texture would be different. The dough was much more moist than I thought it would be. I didn't anticipate the extra liquid from the tomato paste. But as I kneaded and added more flour, it turned into a nice doughball. After a while, it gave me a good windowpane, and I set it aside to rise.

The dough rose up nicely, and I let it go a bit bigger than I usually do. When I decided it was done, it had a rich smell, like a great tomato sauce. Finally, I punched it down and re-rolled it into a boule. I sprinkled about a teaspoon of additional basil and oregano onto a plate and spread it around. Then, I brushed the top of my new boule with olive oil. Finally, I turned the dough over onto the herbs and pressed the dough onto the plate. When I rolled it off, there was a nice coating of shredded herbs stuck to the ball. I put it bottom side down into a well-oiled bowl and let it sit to proof.

Right away after that, I lit up some coals. When those were white, I placed the oiled Dutch oven on and under the right amount of coals. I let that sit to preheat for about another 15 minutes.

When the bread had fully proofed and the Dutch oven was hot, I took the bowl with the boule out to the oven. I lifted up the lid and then, with my hands, carefully lifted the doughball out of the bowl and into the oven, herb side up. I sliced it with an "X" and closed up the lid.

Another 15–20 minutes later, I turned the Dutch oven and lifted the lid just quick enough to insert the thermometer. I was hit with a wave of delicious tomato smell. It was amazing! I knew this bread was going to be good.

After another 20 minutes or so, I checked and the bread was done. The thermometer read about 200 degrees. I turned the bread onto a cooling rack. The smell was wonderful. Later that evening, as we tasted the bread with marinara pasta and meatballs, the meal was complete!

Garlic and Black Pepper Bread

Here's a bread I did on the same day and at the same time as the tomato bread. This was inspired by my good friend Omar Alvarez. He's an amazing Dutch oven chef in his own right, having won the International Dutch Oven World Championship Cook-Off a few years ago. He emailed me his recipe after posting pictures on his Facebook page, and I wanted to try it. I saw that it was close to my core recipe, so I just adapted it!

TOOLS

12-inch Dutch oven

14–15 coals below

18–22 coals above

INGREDIENTS

2 Tbsp. olive oil

3–4 cloves garlic, minced

2 tsp. fresh ground black pepper

1 Tbsp. yeast

2 cups hot water

2 Tbsp. sugar

about 5 cups fresh bread flour

1 tsp. salt

more oil and black pepper for the topping

This process is essentially the same as the tomato bread recipe (page 127). I started by letting the oil steep the garlic and the black pepper (what an aroma *that* is). Then I proofed the yeast in the 110-degree water and the sugar. In a bowl, I sifted all but one cup of flour and added the salt. Then I added the oil/herb mixture and the yeast mixture, and I stirred the ingredients together. I kneaded the dough until it passed the windowpane test and then let it rise.

In this case, I also coated the top of the loaf with more oil and ground black pepper, just like I did the herbs in the tomato bread.

The coals were heated as the bread proofed, and both this bread and the tomato bread baked side by side.

I actually liked the subtleties of the garlic even more than the tomato. But they were both delicious and unique. The whole experience shows how easy it is to make a loaf of bread that's brand new!

Decorative Bread

Here's another approach to creativity. When I was a little kid, one of our erstwhile Christmas traditions was to do bread sculptures. Mom would make a basic variant of a French bread dough, and after it had risen, we would shape it into Santa faces or Christmas trees or lots of other options. Sometimes Mom would make up a big batch of dough, and we'd make six or seven fairly big Santas, and then we'd deliver them to some special friends.

I mentioned that memory to my mom in a phone call one day. We laughed and reminisced about it, and then I asked her for the recipe, which she rattled off from memory. I jotted it down. (It became the core recipe I now use.)

I really wanted to try something like that in my Dutch ovens. I started to think about how to make it work in the circular shape of the oven. I decided on some other designs instead of a Santa—a sun and a moon shape.

Here's how it happened.

TOOLS

2 (12-inch) Dutch ovens

14–15 coals below (each)

18–22 coals above (each)

INGREDIENTS

3 cups hot water

2 Tbsp. yeast

3 Tbsp. sugar

8 cups bread flour

½ Tbsp. salt

1½ Tbsp. oil

2 eggs

I started by increasing the amounts in Mom's original recipe by half. I figured that the basic recipe wouldn't be enough but that doubling the recipe would be too much. I wanted to do 2 Dutch ovens' worth.

I mixed the 110-degree water, the yeast, and the sugar first, and I let that sit for about 10 minutes while I gathered the other ingredients. As always, I reduced the amount of flour in the starting mix and added more in the kneading. I also sifted the flour. Sometimes I do that, and other times I don't, by my whim. I think sifting aerates the flour and makes it a little fluffier.

I mixed the flour, salt, and oil with the yeast mixture and stirred it all up. I turned the dough out onto the floured tabletop and kneaded, sprinkling on more flour. Once the dough made a nice windowpane, I tucked it into a ball, oiled the bowl, and put the doughball in. I also sprayed oil on the doughball and then covered it with a towel, to rise.

Once the dough had risen, I turned the big doughball out onto my floured tabletop, with two Dutch ovens sprayed with oil next to it. (Remember: Mise en place.) At this point, I lit up the coals.

Then I cut the dough into quarters. I spread a layer of dough all around the bottom of the Dutch oven, almost like a pizza crust (but without the rim). That would be my "canvas."

Then I built the image on top of that. I spread some beaten egg wash to use as glue. I started with the sun: I made a round circle in the middle for the face. Then I rolled the flares like clay snakes in between my hands.

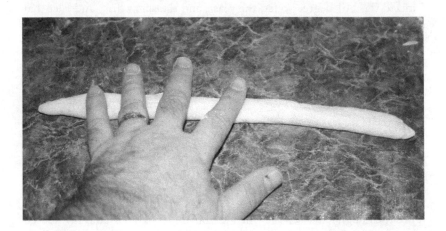

Another few snakes made the eyebrows, the nose, and the smile. A couple of balls, with a deep poke in the center with a finger, made the eyes.

Some more snakes, torn short, made the sunshine rays.

Then I made the moon. I shaped a crescent and then did an eyebrow, a nose, some lips, and an eye with dough. I also added a couple of stars to the left of the crescent.

I went out and poured a lot of coals on both lids, to preheat. While they were preheating, I left the dough art in the Dutch ovens to rise.

Once they'd risen a little bit more and the lids were good and hot, I beat up a couple of eggs and spread them liberally all over the sculptures to help the thinner bits stay on. The egg was the "glue" that held it all together, and it made a rich, shiny, brown crust as well. Then I put the Dutch ovens on and under the coals. I marked the time and went inside to rest.

It wasn't freezing that day, but it wasn't exactly warm either. So after about 15 minutes, I rotated the Dutch ovens and added some coals—a couple on the bottom and much more on top. I lifted the ovens and tapped the ash off the coals on the bottom. I did the same with the coals on top. I also inserted a short-stemmed thermometer.

Another 15–20 minutes and the decorated bread was done! I pulled them off and put them on cooling racks.

I was excited with the results! They made a beautiful central focus at my bread party! It was difficult, however, convincing my guests to eat them!

WRAPUP

Really, after thousands and thousands of years of making breads, you'd think bakers would run out of ideas. And is anything truly new? Maybe not, but I can keep on inventing things I've never tried before, and then (if you'll pardon the pun) I can keep it fresh!

Chapter 8
Wild Yeast and Sourdough Bread

HERE I am, writing this chapter intro, and I'm munching on some sourdough bread. There's little I like more than a couple of slices of good tangy sourdough. Sometimes I like it plain, other times with a slice or two of cheddar. Honestly, I don't do sourdough as much as I could, or even should, but when I do, it's great comfort food.

Eating a fresh-baked sourdough loaf also represents a real accomplishment. Getting it good and getting it right is not easy. When the magic happens, savor it.

There are as many misunderstandings and misconceptions about sourdough as there are about bread baking overall. Is it a wild yeast? Is it a commercial yeast? What makes it tang? How do you catch it? How do you feed it? How do you care for it? Everyone has an answer, and they all think their answer is the only right one.

I've tried a lot of different methods and recipes, and I've discovered quite a few variations. Even still, I've only scratched the surface. I've learned that the more I learn, the more there is to know. In that sense, the more I know, the less I know!

Here I'll share some of the methods and tricks that I've learned.

I've set up this chapter in three sections, labeled "Good," "Better," and "Best." The "Good" section is for a relatively quick and easy sourdough bread that will only take two days total. It might not have quite the depth of flavor as the others, but it will be good and not a lot of work.

In the "Better" section, I'll talk about catching your own wild yeast and working up a delicious flavor. Start to finish, this will take you a week or so and will get you a tasty, tangy loaf as well as a starter that you can keep.

Finally, the "Best" option takes the most time but yields the best results. This is a program of maintaining a starter and cooking sourdough bread over the course of a couple of months, to develop the most possible flavor from the yeast, bacteria, flour, and water that you can! It's easy, but it takes time and patience. Lots of time and patience. But hey, you're in the 2 percent, aren't you?

GOOD:
A (RELATIVELY) QUICK AND EASY SOURDOUGH RECIPE

In this recipe, you create the starter by making a happy environment for yeast growth, and then you seed it with commercial yeast. Letting it sit overnight gives the other flavorful bacteria a chance to grow as well. Then there's a mix with a preferment sponge, which then gets mixed into the final dough. Since there's not as much time for the dough to develop as many natural flavors, I've added some enrichments to help it along.

Quick Sourdough Bread

TOOLS

12-inch Dutch oven

12–14 coals below

22–26 coals above

INGREDIENTS

STEP ONE: THE STARTER

1 cup warm (not hot) water

1 cup flour

1 Tbsp. yeast

STEP TWO: THE SPONGE

1 cup warm water

1–2 cups flour

1 cup sourdough starter

1 tablet of vitamin C (optional)

STEP THREE: THE DOUGH

1 cup yogurt

1 cup sponge

2 Tbsp. honey

1 cup water, 115 degrees

1 Tbsp. salt

3 Tbsp. olive oil

4–5 cups flour, with more for kneading

I start out (pun maliciously intended) by making the starter: I mix the water and all but one cup of flour together and then stir in the yeast. Pretty simple. This is late the night before bake day. I set that aside in a bowl to grow. When I wake up in the morning, it's a frothy and bubbly goo. That mostly means that the yeast has multiplied, but there are also some other bacteria growing as well.

Then I make the sponge. This is the preferment stage. It's basically adding more water and flour to some of the starter. Pretty simple again. The sponge should have a firmer texture than the starter, though. Where the starter looks more like a cake batter, the sponge is more like a loose biscuit dough. It's definitely not as firm as a regular kneaded dough.

Sometimes, I'll take a small tablet of vitamin C and grind it up under a spoon. That gets mixed into the sponge. (A bit of vitamin C can accelerate yeast growth.)

I set the sponge aside to ferment, at room temperature. I also pull the yogurt (from the next set of ingredients) from the fridge and set it aside to get to room temperature.

About 4 hours later, the sponge looks like it has doubled or so in bulk. Time to mix the dough!

I add all the final ingredients together and stir them up with a stout wooden spoon. I put about ½ cup of flour onto my kitchen countertop and dump the dough out onto it. Then I knead and flour, knead and flour, over and over, until the dough stops being so sticky and starts feeling like a smooth dough. That gets it ready for the windowpane test.

Once the dough passes the windowpane test, I shape it into a ball, spray it with oil, and set it aside in a bowl, covered with either a cloth towel or plastic wrap. It takes another 3–4 hours to rise to double in bulk.

At that point, I punch the dough down and reshape it into a ball again. I set it in the oiled Dutch oven and set it aside to proof.

Then I light up the coals. After they have white edges, I pour about 25 coals onto the lid and let it preheat. After 15–20 minutes, I put another 12–14 coals in a ring and set the Dutch oven on them. I slice the top of the now-proofed bread and close up the lid.

After 15 minutes or so, I rotate the lid and the Dutch oven on the coals and then open it to check on the bread and insert the thermometer. Keep the lid open as little as possible. In another 15–20 minutes, check the temperature and rotate the Dutch oven again. You're shooting for an internal temperature of 190–200 degrees. When it gets there, take the coals off the lid and upend the bread (use gloves or hot pads, of course) onto a cooling rack.

I remember baking this and serving it to visitors. Even a lady who swore she didn't like sourdough bread loved it. Of course, it didn't really have a harsh sourness; it was there, but not as edgy. It wasn't a San Francisco–kinda sour. It was still quite yummy, though!

BETTER:
CATCHING A WILD YEAST, AND A THREE-DAY LOAF

Once for a dinner party I cooked an entire seven-course meal entirely in my Dutch ovens. I was cooking the entire day, and it was a lot of fun. I invited a bunch of friends over for the evening. The bread course was, of course, sourdough, and during the dinner, I bragged that the yeast for the sourdough was wild caught.

Everybody looked at me for a moment, then busted out laughing. I didn't get what was so funny, so I asked.

My friend described his mental image of me in khakis and a pith helmet, hacking through the tumbleweeds with a machete, a pack and a gun slung over my shoulder, stalking the wild yeast germs. "There's one. Crikey! He's a big one. He'll sure put up a fight."

Sheesh.

Some people just don't get it.

Anyway, for some it may be fine to let a commercial yeast sit out overnight or to get a starter from a friend. But I think it's more fun and more flavorful to catch your own. It does take some effort and patience, but this is rewarded.

Here's the story of one time that I caught wild yeast and made a three-day, four-step loaf of incredible bread with it. This was several years ago, and at the time, I had some other cool breakthroughs in my "bread-ucation."

Great Dutch Oven Sourdough
...And What I Learned Making It

I've done sourdough breads before, but none of them had that strong tang I was looking for. I made some wonderful loaves, and people would say, "I don't really like sourdough, but I love this bread." Of course, that wasn't really what I wanted to hear. I wanted to be able to taste it and have it zing in my mouth.

This one gave me the zing!

The success was not at all in the recipe, either, but in the process, and that is what I learned.

I began by studying *The Bread Baker's Apprentice* by Peter Reinhart. This is truly an amazing book. I would strongly recommend it for anyone who is wanting to learn how to bake bread, even if you're going to bake it in a Dutch oven instead of a conventional or even a commercial oven, as the book describes.

This recipe had a lot of stages. Even though a lot of time was spent making this (about a week and a half total), and even though I didn't fully understand the need for each stage, I followed each stage faithfully, from starter to barm to sponge to dough. I learned that the long ferment times in each stage gave the bacteria time to develop the flavor. The flavor, I've learned, comes from both the natural yeast (which develops the bready flavors) and the other bacteria that grow and live in the bread (creating the acidy tang). Long fermentation times allow both flavors to deepen to their fullest.

Okay, so here we go:

STEP 1: THE STARTER

INGREDIENTS

flour

warm water

First we catch the wild yeast. I began by putting an amount (I used about 1 cup) of flour in a plastic (or other nonmetal) bowl, along with an equal amount of relatively warm water. It doesn't matter if you use bread flour or all-purpose. I stirred it up and adjusted the mix until it was pretty goopy, almost runny. I set the bowl aside, uncovered, in a prominent and visible place in the kitchen and alerted all in the house that it was *not* to be thrown away, no matter how gross it looked.

For the rest of the days until I caught the germs, every time I walked past it I grabbed a fork and stirred it up. This helped to mix in the crust that formed on the top.

Once a day I fed the starter. By that I mean that I scooped out about half the gunk that was the starter and rinsed it down the drain. Then I added another amount of flour and water, just like before, and stirred the whole thing up. I did this for several days. I kept seeing a few bubbles form, which I thought meant the mixture was getting germy, but it wasn't much. I assumed that it was just the rising air bubbles that were formed when I stirred it up.

Finally, day after day, the perseverance paid off. One morning it was bubbly. Not just a few bubbles, but frothy. To give it extra time, I fed it the same as I had done each day before and gave it one more overnight. I had caught my seed culture and made my starter. That was on Friday.

STEP 2: THE BARM

The barm is another step of fermentation. I'm honestly not sure what the difference is or why this step exists, but I did it anyway. I'm sure that the long fermentation times have a lot to do with it.

INGREDIENTS

1½ cups bread flour

about 1 cup starter

about 1 cup warm water (enough to make it goopy and gooey)

I mixed these ingredients in a bowl on Saturday morning, which I covered with plastic wrap. By afternoon the mixture was expanded and bubbly. I let it go a bit longer, into the evening, and I stirred it up again. Now it was ready for the sponge stage. If I'd had more days, I would have put this mixture into the fridge overnight and made the sponge the next day. But the next day was Sunday, which was when I'd planned to bake the bread. So, after much internal debate, I had to shorten the time. The rest of the starter, by the way, went into the fridge, covered.

STEP 3: THE SPONGE (A.K.A. THE FIRM STARTER)

⅔ cup barm

1 cup bread flour

about ¼ cup warm water (maybe more—enough to make a basic dough texture)

I mixed these ingredients together in a bowl, stirring until all of the flour was combined in and the mixture was forming into a ball. I didn't knead it, but I did end up mixing it with my hands a bit to add some more moisture and make sure it was incorporated. I covered it in plastic wrap and put it aside, letting it ferment for a few more hours, until bedtime. At that point, I put it in the fridge for a long, slow, and cool overnight rise.

STEP 4: THE DOUGH

On Sunday morning I took the sponge out of the fridge and set it aside to come closer to room temperature. I dumped it out onto my floured countertop and, using my bread cutter/scraper, cut it into 10–12 equal-sized chunks. While those were still warming up, I got these other ingredients together into the bowl:

INGREDIENTS

4 cups bread flour

2 tsp. salt

1¾ cups water, 110 degrees

the chunks of the sponge

I mixed all of these ingredients together and dumped it all out onto the tabletop and began kneading. As always, I added flour as I went to make it the right consistency (not too sticky, not too stiff and dry). After about 15 minutes, it passed the windowpane test, and I kneaded a few more minutes just to be sure. I oil-sprayed the bowl and set the ball to rise.

A few hours later, the dough had doubled in bulk (or so), and I pulled it out and shaped it into a boule.

Now, this is where I did things a bit differently than I did before. I had some cloth, which I sprayed with oil and dusted with flour. I draped that cloth over a bowl and set the dough boule into the middle of the cloth. I folded the cloth over the top of the dough and set it aside to proof. You'll see why in a bit.

STEP 5: THE LOAF

After the dough had been rising for a few hours, I began preparing the Dutch oven. I lit up a lot of coals, and let them get nice and white on the edges. I oiled the Dutch oven and set it up with 14–16 coals underneath and 26–30 coals on top. That's right, I wanted it to be *hot*.

After 15–20 minutes, when I could see that the oven was hot and the bread was nicely proofed in the bowl, it was all ready. I brought the dough out to the oven, set the Dutch oven lid aside, and upended the bowl, dropping the dough into the Dutch oven. Quickly, I pulled off the cloth, made some slices in the top of the dough (which was the bottom a few moments ago), and closed up the lid.

See, the whole "cloth in the bowl" thing made for easy transfer of the proofed bread to the fully preheated Dutch oven. I didn't have to mess with parchment, and there was no lag time heating up the base of the Dutch oven or the air inside.

After about 15 minutes, I rotated the lid and the Dutch oven and then replenished some of the coals, top and bottom. I was careful on the bottom coals—I added some, but I'm always cautious in how many I add. In this case, I put on four, one on each "side." Too many bottom coals can make for a heavy bottom crust. I also lifted the lid and inserted the thermometer.

In another 15–20 minutes, I checked again, and they were done, at 200 degrees. The top crust didn't brown much, so I wasn't sure if it was done, but the thermometer said it was, so I brought the oven in. I dropped the bread out of the Dutch oven and onto the cooling rack. The thermometer came out pretty clean, which was a good sign. I let the bread cool for a couple of hours.

The bread, when I finally cut into it, was soft and delicious. The crusts were soft and the bread was chewy, tasty, and done all the way through. It was perfect. Like I said before, it was easily the best sourdough bread I've ever made.

Here are the things that I learned:

First of all, a long process of multiple steps of fermentation helps all of the rich, complex flavors develop. Taking your time and not rushing this process is worth it. Look at the ingredients—there's nothin' there. No egg, no sugar, no oils, no herbs. It's essentially you, the wheat, and the germs. Yet, if you let nature take its sweet time, you'll get some seriously delicious bread.

Second, preheating the entire Dutch oven made a big difference in the baking. The cloth with the bowl made this easy and practical.

This was definitely a major breakthrough in my bread baking education.

I've incorporated many of the things I learned for this recipe into much of my regular bread baking routine: whenever possible, I preheat the entire oven, and I only do "pot proofs," where I preheat the lid, for rolls or loaves with a special shape. With those, where you can't really lift them into a hot oven, you have to let them proof in the bottom of the Dutch oven and only preheat the lid.

I don't use the same cloth technique, but I have a couple of proofing baskets that are cloth lined. They work great. The cloth in this recipe worked great too, but using a cloth-lined basket is more rustic.

Once you've baked the bread, you have a few options as to what to do with that fermented goo that you used to start the whole process. One option is to throw it out with the garbage or to rinse it down your sink. Another option is to put a lid on it and put it in your fridge. About every week or two, pull it out and refresh it. You do this by dumping about half of it out and mixing in more flour and water, in equal parts. Then put it back in your fridge. We'll talk about storage a little later in this chapter.

A third option is to keep going and make your starter even better!

BEST:
CULTIVATING A UNIQUE AND DELICIOUS STARTER

Okay, recruits. Are you ready to take it to the next level? Are you truly one of the 2 percent? Are you committed to baking the best bread possible? Are you prepared to take that commitment to places that border on the obsessive? Is your family ready to have you committed?

In this section, I'll show you how to make sourdough more like the pros do, even though you're not baking hundreds of loaves a day. Creating a starter that will serve you well will take time and dedication. Here's what you'll commit to:

- Create a starter, or use the one you made in the previous section.

- Feed that starter daily for at least sixty days

- Use that starter to bake a loaf of sourdough bread at least once a week during those sixty days.

- Preserve the starter in your fridge or freezer

- Share your bread, your starter, and your knowledge with others

That's a lot to do. Fortunately, even though cultivating a starter takes dedication, it's also pretty forgiving. If you keep going, you'll reap the rewards with delicious, chewy, and tangy breads.

Ready, then? Let's get started.

To start off, choose a container of either plastic, glass, ceramic, or some similar material (a non-reactive metal). The container should have a lid because the stuff inside is going to get ripe. Also, the container should have a capacity of about one quart and should have a pretty wide opening. I use a tall, square plastic storage container.

1: CREATE a sourdough starter using the instructions on page 142. Put it out each day, uncovered. Keep the container out of reach of pets or small children on an open countertop. Each day, pour half of it out and add fresh flour and water back in. Keep doing that until it bubbles and froths, in a big way. The mixture should double in bulk. If your container is transparent, you should be able to see bubbles along the sides all the way from the top to the bottom. That means you caught your yeast germs.

Keep doing this replenishing process for a week to develop the other germs too. These are the germs that bring the tangy flavor. While you're in this process, show everyone in your household the container with the starter, and tell them that no matter how gross it looks, nor how badly it smells, it is *not* to be thrown away. It's safe to use for breads. Reassure them that the lid will keep the smell contained.

At the end of that first week, make a loaf of sourdough bread, just like before. This, by the way, will help win your family over to your side. They will be so amazed at the rich, wonderful flavor of your bread that they will encourage you. Especially when you promise them that the bread will keep getting better. And better.

2: AT the end of the day when you make the barm for that first loaf, refresh the starter again. This time, set it aside on your countertop with the lid on and sealed.

Then, every day, or at least every other day, refresh the starter. I do this with all-purpose flour, by the way. Bread flour's more expensive, and you don't need any gluten for this step. Probably midway through that week, the starter will start to develop a really strong odor when you take off the lid. That's good. That means the germs are developing some good, rich flavors.

At the very least, at the end of the week, use the starter to bake another loaf. Follow the procedure exactly as before: starter, barm, sponge, dough, loaf.

3: THIS is where the persistence will begin to pay off. Make another loaf of sourdough every week. Every day or two, refresh the starter. All the time it sits on your countertop at room temperature. Each time you refresh it, over the next few hours or day, it should swell up with a new round of frothy goo.

As the weeks go by, you should notice that your loaves are becoming richer, more flavorful, and more complex. You can add some variety if you like, like with some other flavors or enrichments, but really it's the tang that'll getcha! And that tang becomes better and better with each loaf.

4: FINALLY, after about two months of this process, your starter will have found a nice, rich, exciting, and consistent flavor. That's quite an accomplishment. You'll have a true work of culinary art. Your patience, diligence, and dedication will have produced a treasure.

Now, if you want, you could just continue with this, refreshing and baking, forever. Really, that's what professional bakeries do. They use and refresh their starter daily.

Or, if it's time to rest, you can store the starter. Refresh it one more time, close the lid, and put it in the fridge. Label it so nobody confuses it with some ugly, moldy leftovers and throws it away.

From then on, you should refresh it about once a week. I say "should" because it could be done as little as every other week. However, the longer you go between refreshings the greater the likelihood that the yeast will eventually starve and die. If you haven't refreshed the starter for a while, especially after a few weeks, you might see a layer of slightly murky liquid on the top. It might smell like alcohol . . . because that's what it is. Alcohol is, in fact, the by-product of the yeast life cycle. (This is why dough rising is called "fermentation.") You can simply pour this stuff into the sink.

When you do want to bake a loaf of good, rich sourdough, pull out your starter and awaken it by refreshing it and leaving it overnight on the counter, covered, as before. Then, continue on with the process. The original mother starter gets refreshed and put back in the fridge.

LONG-TERM STORAGE AND SHARING

Suppose that, after spending two months of feeding your family sourdough bread week after week, day after day, month after month, they get a little tired of its edgy goodness, and they want to try some other kind of bread. Let's say that after all that focused dedication and effort, you're so sick of sourdough bread that you cancel your vacation to San Francisco and you are tempted to fling your starter into the back yard while shouting, "Be FREEEEE!" Or maybe you wake up at night with horrible dreams of a terrifying tan blob that reeks of acid and alcohol growing out of your kitchen and swallowing all in its fermented path of destruction! Yeah. It's time to take a break.

My point is that maybe you might not want to bake sourdough every week or even every three or four weeks. What if you want to do it every three to four months, or longer? One option, of course, is to keep track of that starter in the fridge. Keep refreshing it, week after week, month after month.

"Wait. How long ago did I refresh this thing last? How long has it been here? Wow, that's a lot of hooch on top. Oh, oh, I think I killed it." That's a pretty sad tale considering how much time and effort went into creating that wonderful starter in the first place.

Here's one way to do some long-term storage of your yeast germs.

First, bake one more delicious loaf of bread. Make the recipe one and a half times the original, or maybe even double. Do the whole process: you know, starter, barm, sponge, dough, loaf. This time, however, when you're in the last phase, there's an extra step. First, make the loaf without any enrichments. Just simple, four-ingredient sourdough. Knead it as normal, and let it rise. When you dump it out to shape it, however, cut out the extra. By that I mean, if you doubled the recipe, cut away half of it. If you did it one and a half times the original, then cut away a third. Shape the remaining loaf as normal and set it aside to proof and then, eventually, to bake.

Now you've got a big hunk of dough in front of you. Using your hands or your dough cutter, make the dough into doughballs about the size of a golf ball, maybe slightly larger. Set them on a lightly oiled cookie sheet. When you've got six to twelve of them on the sheet, cover it in plastic wrap and put it, level, into the freezer. Three to four hours later, take the tray out and gather the now rock-hard, frozen-in-time samples of bacterial goodness into zip-top baggies (try and evacuate as much air as possible) and mark the date on them. Put them back in the freezer. They will keep, suspended, for months.

Then, when you want to have great sourdough again, go to the freezer. Look behind the leftover casseroles and the boxes of Hot Pockets and TV dinners until you find your treasured sourdough balls. Take a couple out of a bag and re-close it. Set them in a bowl on your countertop for three to four hours to thaw and one to two more hours to wake up and rise, like little dinner rolls. They might not double in bulk, but they should swell up just fine.

Then add a cup of all-purpose flour and one to one and a half cups of warm water to the bowl. Stir it all up and let it sit overnight. If all went well, you should have a bubbly starter in the morning. Refresh it and let it go again, to be sure and to develop more flavor. From there, you're back to your original recipe and your original process. If you start to run out of the frozen doughballs, simply make another batch of dough and make more doughballs.

Another cool thing you can do once the doughballs are frozen is to give them away. If you have friends who love sourdough but who you know won't go through all the months-long effort needed to make a delicate and complex starter, you can share your culinary wealth with them. You can dress it up however you like: in fancy jars with ribbons, with the balls individually wrapped in colored cellophane wrap, or simply in a zip-top baggie as they are. Include a small piece of paper for instructions.

RECIPES

Here are some other recipes that use sourdough starters and techniques.

Enriched Sourdough

I remember one time, when I was practicing making breads, I finally made a loaf of bread with a nice crust and a fluffy, soft crumb. It rose nicely. I did it based on the instructions in *The Baking Book* by Lloyd Moxon, just like I'd done previously. But this time I made a few changes. At the time, I wasn't sure which change was the key or if they were all keys together, but the recipe worked out.

The first change from the original sourdough bread recipe was adding an egg. Not exactly a revelation, but at the time I was beginning to understand the role of enrichments and their impact on the crumb.

Another change was that I had just discovered the windowpane test and had begun to knead enough to create the gluten strands. I'd finally discovered the key to getting a good rise, and it was in the kneading.

The last breakthrough was learning to preheat the Dutch oven. As I've said before, the bread needs to hit the heat immediately. This creates the initial spring in the loaf. If you're heating up your Dutch oven gradually, the bread will cook but it won't blossom and swell right at the beginning and then caramelize, bake, and set into place. Now I always preheat, at least the lid, but back then it was something new! At the time, I only had hints that it would help, so I decided to try it.

Anyway, here's the recipe:

TOOLS

12-inch Dutch oven

10–12 coals below

18–22 coals above

INGREDIENTS: THE SPONGE (STEP ONE)

1 cup sourdough starter (see page 142)

2½ cups hot water

4 cups flour

INGREDIENTS: THE DOUGH (STEP TWO)

1 cup flour (with as much as 2–3 more cups during kneading)

1 egg

2 Tbsp. sugar

3 Tbsp. oil

1 Tbsp. salt

The night before baking, I made the starter. I took a few globs of goo from the starter I had in the fridge and mixed it with equal amounts of flour and water. I needed enough new goo to make a cup full of starter. By morning it was good and frothy with lots of good yeast bugs.

So before I headed off to work, I mixed all the ingredients in the sponge step in a bowl and stirred it up with a wooden spoon (metal utensils react with the yeast). I covered the bowl with plastic and set it aside. Then I went off to work. You know, at my job. Earning my living . . . my daily bread.

After I got home, I mixed the dough ingredients into the mixture in the bowl. Then I turned the dough out onto a floured tabletop and started kneading, adding flour as I went. As long as the bread was too sticky, I kept adding flour and kneading it into a ball.

Every once in a while, I did the windowpane test. I grabbed a piece of the dough, flattened it, and stretched it out into a translucent "windowpane." The first few times, it shredded and tore quickly. That meant that the gluten hadn't developed enough yet, and the dough needed more kneading. Finally, the dough pulled without tearing, and I knew that it was ready. This was the first time I truly knew how long to knead dough. I liked having a solid guide instead of just a clock.

Then I sprayed oil in the bowl and put in the doughball. I sprayed the doughball with oil as well and set it aside to rise. Then I rested. At least, as much as my kids would allow.

After a couple of hours, I could see that the dough had risen. I was quite surprised by how much it had risen because usually it takes sourdough much longer to rise. I wonder if having better developed gluten made it more flexible and able to expand. Hmmm . . .

Then I punched the dough down and reshaped it into a single boule. I sprayed oil in the Dutch oven and put the doughball inside. I cut three slashes in the top of the dough, and I set it aside to proof.

Then I lit up a buncha coals. Once those were white, I brought out the lid and put 24–26 coals on the lid. About 10 minutes later, I could tell the lid was really hot, and the dough in the Dutch oven had risen a little more. I put the Dutch oven out on some coals and put the lid on top, using the right amount of coals for top and bottom (see beginning of recipe). Then baking was simply a matter of keeping the Dutch oven hot and rotating it every 15 minutes or so.

I baked the bread for about 40 minutes. I put a thermometer in, which read about 190 degrees. Not bad, eh?

Oh, another thing I did differently from the original recipe was to let the sourdough bread cool before cutting it. I'd read that this step is important to finish the cooking, so I set the bread on a cooling rack. Once it was cooled (but still a bit warm), I cut it and was amazed. The crumb was light and flaky, and the crust wasn't too hard. It was a great sourdough bread and made for a delicious sandwich loaf.

Sourdough Rye Bread

Most of the time, I like to cook for others. I like to cook things that they like. Then, when I pull it off and they tell me how great it tastes, I feel good, you know? It's a win-win.

I'm sure this has some connection to my deep-seated need for validation and praise, and it probably stems from something my parents did wrong when I was young. Trust me, it's their fault I need therapy.

But once in a while, I like to cook something just for me. Like that Palestinian dish, kofta bi tahini. I don't care if the rest of the family doesn't like it. I do, and I'm gonna cook it and eat it all myself!

See, one thing my dad did (right) for me is show me how incredibly good a sandwich you can make with three basic components: rye bread, braunsch-weiger, and baby Swiss cheese. I love those sandwiches. But my wife hates them. She even hates me after I eat them. Well, specifically she hates my breath after I eat them.

Some days, when my dear wife is out traveling for work, I'll bake a dark rye bread so all that week I can have various sandwiches at my work, one of which will be, of course, the dreaded "schwiegermeister." Oh, yes. It will be yummy. It will make my lunch time worth living for.

TOOLS

12-inch Dutch oven

10–12 coals below

18–20 coals above

INGREDIENTS: THE SPONGE

1 cup sourdough starter (see page 142)

2 cups dark rye flour

2 cups white bread flour

1 cup plain yogurt

1½ cups warm water

2 Tbsp. vital wheat gluten

1 Tbsp. dough enhancer (optional)

INGREDIENTS: THE DOUGH

1 egg

2 Tbsp. molasses

3 Tbsp. oil

1 Tbsp. salt

2 Tbsp. Postum

liberal shakes of caraway seeds

1 cup bread flour (plus as much as another cup during kneading)

I started by activating the starter the night before baking. I poured out what I had left of the starter into a bowl and added about a cup of water (sort of hot to the touch) and a cup of flour. That was early in the evening. By later that night, the starter was starting to foam up.

I'd like to say that, as a point of pride (another big psychological issue of mine), I used wild-caught sourdough yeast, not commercial yeast. See, if you use yeast from a jar, then what you're really doing is cultivating a culture of commercial yeast. The fact that you leave it out overnight doesn't change the fact that it's still a commercial yeast.

On the other hand, if you get a starter from leaving out flour and water and you catch yeast from the air, then it's a truer sourdough, and I think it tastes better.

(I also need to comment on the dough enhancer. This is an interesting ingredient that my friend over at mormonfoodie.com turned me on to. It's got a bunch of interesting things in it that make dough rise up better and have better structure. I'm not convinced it's absolutely necessary, but I've been experimenting with it lately, and I'm not *un*impressed. Also, I added vital wheat gluten because rye flour doesn't have the gluten content that wheat flour does. I've found that it makes a big difference.)

Anyway, once the sourdough starter was bubbling a bit, I put a cup of it in a bowl and added in all of the remaining first set of ingredients to make the sponge. I don't know why it's called that, other than that once it rises up and ferments, it does have a certain sponginess, I guess.

I set the sponge aside and let it ferment not only overnight but much of the next day as well, as my crazy schedule allowed.

When I got back home, it had fermented up nicely. I added all of the second set of ingredients. The cup of flour helped the dough to not be quite so sticky on the table, even though I also added more as I was kneading.

I kneaded for 15 minutes or so, until the dough passed the windowpane test, and then sprayed a bowl with oil and set it in. I coated the dough with spray oil and covered the bowl with plastic.

The dough rose for 1–1½ hours. Then I punched it down, shaped it, and put it in the oiled Dutch oven to proof. I scored the dough with three slashes across the top.

While the dough was proofing, I got the coals going. Once the coals were hot enough, I put the requisite amount on the lid to preheat it. That sat for about 15 minutes, and then I put the Dutch oven with the sourdough bread dough on the coals and set the lid on.

A little past halfway through the bake time, I stuck thermometer in the bread and closed the lid up again. I baked it until the thermometer read about 190 degrees. (I like the bread a little softer, with not such a hard crust. It can really go up to 200 degrees and be fine, since it's a darker loaf.)

Then it was done. I let it cool, cut it, and made a sandwich. *Mmmmmmm!*

Chapter 9
Quick Breads

WE'VE SPENT pages and pages so far talking about yeast breads, and rightly so. It's a complex and challenging process that I've struggled to learn.

Now let's turn our attention to another kind of bread, leavened not with germs but with chemicals. We call them "quick breads" because they don't take hours or days to get the lift and fluff. It's important, however, to realize that they are different kinds of breads. They taste different, the texture is different, and the method is different. At first, this process was difficult for me because I tried to make quick breads with a yeast bread mentality. It wasn't until I separated the two types in my mind that I was able to make good quick breads.

Let me say this clearly: Quick breads and yeast breads are two completely separate animals.

Flour and water, by themselves, make for flat, tough breads. Essentially, you get a cracker. When you add in bubbles, even tiny ones, magical things happen. When the bread is baking, the heat expands those bubbles, adding lift to the dough. Then, the heat sets the flour and water into a structure around those bubbles, and it all stays nice and poofy. So where do those bubbles come from? Well in a yeast bread, the bubbles are CO_2 from the yeast germs, feeding and belching. In a sponge cake, the bubbles are aerated in by whipping up the egg whites. In quick breads, the CO_2 comes from a chemical reaction between something acidic and something called an "alkali."

BAKING SODA

If you think back on your elementary school experience, you probably witnessed, at some point, the Baking Soda Volcano of Doom . . . I mean, of Science. This is where someone made a mountain out of aluminum foil or papier-mâché or any of a number of other substances. In the peak was a cup. The demonstrator would pour in either baking soda or vinegar by itself and then add the other afterward. Instantly it would bubble up and foam over the edge of the cup, flowing down the side of the "mountain."

Of course, this didn't really teach you anything about how volcanoes worked, but it might have taught you about chemistry. When you mix an acid and an alkali (also called a "base"), they react and produce CO_2.

Of course, our grandmas have been using this principle to make biscuits and pancakes for years. They might not have known it, but it was true nonetheless. All of the ingredients in the biscuits contribute to the process. The baking soda provides the alkali. The buttermilk provides the acid to react with the alkali. The fat in the buttermilk and the shortening or butter combine with the flour to make a texture that will trap the CO_2 bubbles as they form. Then the liquid in the buttermilk sets with the flour when it bakes to solidify that new, fluffy structure.

That alone would be cool enough, but some issues arise right away. First of all, the moment you mix the soda and the buttermilk, the reaction begins. So the quicker you get it in the oven after mixing, the better. Second, the cooler the fats are when you start, the more gas bubbles they'll be able to trap, so you'll want to avoid working it in your hands and raising the temperature.

That also means you have to make sure your recipe has enough acid in it to react with the soda.

BAKING POWDER

Okay, so baking soda is an alkali. What about baking powder? What's the difference?

Baking powder combines a powdered acid (usually cream of tartar) along with the baking soda. Since they're both powders, they don't begin reacting until they're mixed with a liquid, like water, milk, or egg. Now you don't have to worry about the acid in the recipe—you have it in the powder.

Most modern baking powders are "double acting." That means that in addition to the first acid, there's a second acid that only reacts with the alkali under high heat. So when you mix the dough, it begins reacting right away, and then, as the dough bakes, the heat triggers a second round of reactions and gives even more lift.

FLOUR

Before we dive into some recipes, I should say something about the flour used in quick breads. In a yeast bread, the yeast produces the CO_2, and it's trapped in the gluten strands after you add water, time, and agitation (kneading).

In quick breads, the CO_2 is trapped by the fats mixed into the flour. So there's no kneading, and there's no gluten. As a result, you don't have to use high-protein flours. All-purpose flours work perfectly here!

Self-rising flour, by the way, is an all-purpose flour that has baking powder pre-mixed in. I don't use self-rising flour because if I did, I would be locked into the proportions and composition of the powder the miller chose. I'd rather just mix it all in myself. It's the same principle that I use with garlic salt. I'd rather have garlic powder and salt separately and be able to mix in the amount of each that I want.

PUTTING IT ALL TOGETHER

Let's work first on something we can all see as a good, traditional bread.

Irish Soda Bread

For many years, the one bread that had consistently failed me was Irish soda bread. I'd tried it many times and always failed. Most of the time this bread would turn out like a brick. Sometimes the inner crumb would be fairly soft, but even that was usually pretty dense, and the crust would be like a suit of armor.

I studied and researched and tried hard to figure out why this bread didn't work. I saw many recipes, and many of the ones that looked light and fluffy read more like cake recipes than bread, with lots of sugar and eggs. These recipes didn't seem like the Irish soda bread I was shooting for. Crusty is fine, as long as it's still soft to the teeth. I wanted it to puff up and brown in the oven.

Even after all this study and learning, my soda loaves would still turn out like doorstops—practical, but that didn't make them any more palatable, even with butter and jam.

(I did learn, however, that something similar to a Dutch oven was often used to bake traditional soda bread—big cast-iron pots, or "bastibles," often with sharp bumps on the underside of the lid. When cooking, especially meats, these bumps would be points where the steam would gather and drip back down onto the meat.)

I didn't feel like I could claim any authority as a Dutch oven bread baker if I couldn't do a decent chemically leavened bread. I knew that it *could* be done in a Dutch oven, but I couldn't seem to pull it off.

Then one day, I had some breakthroughs and it all worked. From then on, I was able to consistently make a delicious, light soda bread.

TOOLS

12-inch Dutch oven

10–12 coals below

20–24 coals above

INGREDIENTS

2 full cups all-purpose flour

1 tsp. salt

1 slightly heaping tsp. cream of tartar

1 heaping tsp. baking soda

1 cup (full ½-pint carton) buttermilk

I started by lighting the coals. Once those were showing some good white burn, I set the Dutch oven (with a spritz of oil on the inside) on and under the coals. While the Dutch oven was preheating, I set about making the dough, which goes quickly.

I added all of the dry ingredients together in a bowl. (I sifted in the flour, mainly to aerate it.) Notice, again, that I didn't use bread flour. Use all-purpose here.

Then I made a well in the middle of the mixture, poured in the buttermilk, and gradually stirred it in. Soon it was clumping together. I reached in the bowl with my fingers and kneaded it and shaped it in the bowl. This is an important part: don't work the dough too much. It's *not* a yeast bread, where you knead it for 20 minutes or more. For this recipe, a few squeezes and folds to mix the dough well, and a bit of shaping and molding, and you're ready to go.

I shaped the dough into a disc about 6 inches by about 1½ inches high. This is another important part. I don't know how I missed this, but in the past I always shaped the dough into a ball. A ball has too much mass and won't lift. See? I was thinking like a yeast bread.

I cut a cross pattern on the top of the dough. There are all kinds of stories about why this bread is traditionally cut with a cross on top. I'm kind of a practical guy, so I know why *I* did it. One, the cut allows the bread to spring up and spread. Two, the cut gives the bread a place to vent a lot of the steam during baking. And three, the cross cut makes the bread easy to break into four equal pieces once it's done.

I put the dough into the now-hot Dutch oven and baked it for 30–40 minutes. I recommend baking to an internal temperature of 170–180 degrees. I baked this one to 190 degrees, and it was a little too crusty, I think, especially on the bottom. Resist the urge to add too many coals underneath, by the way. Watch the bottom coals and do some replenishing so they don't burn out, but don't go crazy with it.

In the end, the bread swelled up nicely, smelled wonderful, and tasted great.

Like I said, soda breads and other quick breads are totally different animals from yeast breads. In order for me to successfully make this loaf, I had to separate myself from much of what I had learned about yeast breadmaking and make the soda bread by its own rules.

Drop Biscuits

I actually like drop biscuits a lot because you don't have to handle them much. You mix them, you scoop them out with a spoon, and you drop them into the hot Dutch oven. No folding, no rolling—just simple bready goodness.

TOOLS

12-inch Dutch oven

10 coals below

22 coals above

INGREDIENTS

2 cups all-purpose flour

½ cup unsalted butter, cold, cut into small pieces

1 Tbsp. baking powder

1 tsp. kosher salt

1 cup whole milk

I start by lighting up the coals and lightly oiling the inside of my Dutch oven. When the coals are getting white edges, I put them in a ring and set the lidded Dutch oven on top. I set the remaining coals on the lid and leave it to preheat.

Mixing the ingredients is easy. I start with the flour, and I cut in the butter. The easiest way to cut the butter is with a pastry knife, but I've seen people do it by crisscrossing two butter knives like they're sword fighting themselves and the butter's caught in the middle. *Oh, noooooo!*

You can use your hands to blend the flour and the butter, but then you'll be raising the temperature of the butter, and, remember, we don't want to do that. If you do use your hands, chill the dough for a little bit after mixing.

While I'm doing this chopping and mixing, I add the baking powder and salt. It will all look like a kind of coarse meal. I pour in the milk and stir it all up with my trusty wooden spoon. Actually, since we're not dealing with yeast germs, you could use just about any kind of spoon. But I still like my wooden spoon.

Then I turn to the Dutch oven and remove the lid. I scoop out a spoonful of dough and drop it into the bottom of the oven. It might sizzle a bit. I keep doing that until I either run out of room or out of dough. Usually the latter. Then I put on the lid with the coals and bake the biscuits. I'll check it in about 15 minutes, at which point they are usually done or close to it. Sometimes, however, they need a few more minutes.

When they're nice and golden, take the Dutch oven off the coals and scoop the biscuits out with a plastic spatula and serve them. They can be served right away, or you can wait until other dishes are done and serve them cool. Either way is yummy!

Variation: Garlic Cheddar Drop Biscuits

Here's the best-ever variation on the drop biscuits. I love these with seafood because they take what could be a highbrow esoteric dish and makes it home-cooked comfort food.

INGREDIENTS

2 cups all-purpose flour

½ cup unsalted butter, cold, cut into small pieces

1 Tbsp. baking powder

1 tsp. kosher salt

4–5 garlic cloves, finely minced (or about 1 teaspoon garlic powder)

½ cup grated cheddar

1 cup whole milk

4 Tbsp. melted butter

chopped parsley

The process for prep and cooking is much the same as the previous recipe, with only two exceptions:

One, add the garlic and the cheddar in when mixing the dry ingredients and then stir it all in with the milk, as before.

Two, immediately after pulling the biscuits out of the Dutch oven, brush each one with melted butter and then sprinkle with the chopped parsley. Fresh parsley is best, but dried will do.

Mark's Biscuits and Gravy

The first time I ever had biscuits and gravy was at a Scout camp. Our patrol piled into the mess hall alongside every other patrol one morning, and we were served big bowls full of biscuits. That was cool enough. After the generic nondenominational "grace" was said, everyone but me started grabbing biscuits, tearing them open and laying them out on their plates. I had some biscuits, but I was wondering where the butter and jam was.

Then they started pouring this white gravy all over them. I'd never heard of this before! But it looked really good. So I joined in, and it was amazing. The best breakfast food I'd ever had.

I've included both the gravy and the biscuit recipes here. Working on both parts of the dish and timing them out to be done at about the same time was tricky.

TOOLS

10-inch Dutch oven

15–18 coals below

12-inch Dutch oven

12 coals below

24 coals above

INGREDIENTS: THE GRAVY

½–1 lb. ground breakfast sausage

1 medium onion

2½ Tbsp. flour

½ cup buttermilk

1½ cups milk

a shake or two of:

salt

black pepper

celery salt

parsley

cinnamon

Worcestershire sauce

INGREDIENTS: THE BISCUITS

2 cups all-purpose flour

½ tsp. baking soda

2 tsp. baking powder

2 Tbsp. shortening

1 cup buttermilk

I started by lighting up a lot of coals. I'd need them! I set out the 10-inch Dutch oven with plenty of coals underneath and started cooking the sausage in it. I also chopped up the onion and added that. While that was cooking, I set up the coals for the 12-inch oven to preheat. Then I started mixing the biscuits.

I mixed the dry ingredients and then added the shortening, cutting it all together with a pastry knife. Then I mixed in the buttermilk and continued cutting with the pastry knife. After it was well mixed, I rolled the dough out flat on the floured countertop.

I cut the biscuits into circles using a child's drinking cup. When I had cut out all I could. I wadded up the remaining dough, rolled it out again, and cut more. I put the biscuits in the heated Dutch oven and closed up the lid.

Once the biscuits were in the oven and baking, I mixed the flour into the now-browned sausage and onions in the 10-inch Dutch oven, making a sort of semi-roux with the sausage drippings, and then added the buttermilk, milk, and spices. I left the gravy on the coals to heat up and thicken.

I turned the biscuit oven a time or two, and I think I cooked it a total of 15–20 minutes. The biscuits baked, the gravy thickened, and finally it was time to bring it all in and try it. It was delicious. I knew as I smelled all those spices in the gravy that it was going to be heavenly. I wasn't disappointed.

Whipped Cream Biscuits
with Split Pea & Ham Soup

Every time that I roast a ham, that ham bone stares at me from the back of the fridge. Covered in aluminum foil, in a colorful ceramic bowl, it mocks me: "You never finished me off!"

So one particular day I made an amazing split pea soup! And, of course, split pea soup goes best with fresh biscuits! As a bonus, I've included the entire recipe here.

THE SOUP

TOOLS

12-inch deep Dutch oven

10–17 coals below (Use more when getting a boil going, less when simmering. At times, when getting it boiling, I also had a few coals on top.)

INGREDIENTS

1 ham bone, with lots of meat left on it

1 (1-lb.) bag dried split peas

1 onion, chopped

8 cups water or chicken stock, or any combination of the two

2 stalks celery

1 potato

generous shakes of oregano, thyme, and garlic

liberal amounts of salt and coarse ground pepper to taste

THE WHIPPED CREAM BISCUITS

TOOLS

12-inch shallow Dutch oven

12 coals below

20 coals above

INGREDIENTS

4 cups flour

2 Tbsp. baking powder (not heaping tablespoons, but not level either)

4 tsp. sugar

3 tsp. salt

3 (½-pint) cartons whipping cream

I started with a lot of hot coals, probably around 17 plus, maybe as many as 20, all underneath my deep 12-inch Dutch oven. I put the ham bone in first. The ham bone was left over from a couple of weeks previously. When the soup was all done, there was a hint of the original baste from the ham in the taste. *Mmmmm. . . .*

I added the peas (dry, of course), onion, and water, and set it on the coals, covered. After about 20 minutes or so it was boiling. At that point, managing the heat was interesting. I had to take off enough coals to have the oven simmering but not so many that it just sat there being hot. I can't really tell you how many coals that required—you'll simply have to watch it. I started with about 10, and that number changed both up and down as the coals burned and the soup cooked.

Next, while simmering the soup, I worked on the biscuits. First, I made sure that I had enough fresh charcoal briquettes getting lit in my side fire to bake the biscuits. Once they were lit, I put them under and on the 12-inch Dutch oven and gave the inside a light coating of spray oil.

Next I blended all the dry ingredients into a mixing bowl and then, one by one, stirred in each carton of cream. When that was mixed, I did have to sprinkle on a touch of flour because it was still a little sticky.

Then, I floured my countertop and rolled the dough out to a ¾-inch-thick slab. At the time, I actually got out a tape measure and checked it. If my wife had come out and seem me doing that, she would have laughed her head off. Hey, I didn't know. Now I do.

I used a child's cup to cut the circles. The original recipe said that if you twist the cup, it ruins the biscuits. I was careful not to twist, but I'm not sure how it would ruin them. Something about releasing the air in the dough?

I arranged a bunch of the snug biscuits in the bottom of the heated Dutch oven and set the lid on to bake.

With biscuits baking, I chopped up the celery and diced the potato into a bowl. I mixed all the seasonings (generous and liberal) into that bowl and then dumped it all in the pot. I replenished the coals, making it hot again to boil. Not long after this, I also took off the lid. I was hoping to boil down some of the liquid in the soup. That turned out to be a good idea.

After 15–20 minutes, the biscuits were done. If they're not fully browned on top, you can give them a few more minutes off the coals with more coals only on top.

Everyone seems to like their split pea soup at a different consistency. I just simmered and cooked off the liquid until the potatoes were done and the peas were my kind of consistency.

Then I cut the meat off the bone into the soup and served it. I always eat too much on Sundays. The soup was incredible!

Soda Pop Biscuits

TOOLS

12-inch Dutch oven

8 coals below

17 coals above

INGREDIENTS

3 cups flour

$^3/_8$ cup oil

1 (12-oz.) can 7Up

3 Tbsp. baking powder

The process was pretty simple. First, I got some coals hot, and I put them on and below the empty Dutch oven to preheat it.

Then I mixed all the ingredients in a bowl and stirred. I was careful to keep the ingredients cool and to handle the dough as little as possible. It ended up being a little sticky, so I sprinkled in a little more flour. The dough was so light and airy that I didn't have to roll it out; I could spread it out with my hands on the floured tabletop. I spread the dough to about ¾ inch thick and cut rounds with a drinking cup.

Then I put the dough circles into the preheated oven and started the baking. After 30–40 minutes, I took the Dutch oven off the bottom coals but left the coals on the lid so the tops would brown without the bottoms burning.

When the biscuits were done, they were delicious!

Flaky Biscuits
with Mark's Tomato Soup

Some days you will feel like life, the cosmos, and karma are all conspiring against you. The coals won't stay lit, the storms rage, the winds rush, and it's just plain tough to cook your food. Then the recipe bombs, and you end up with something that is totally unlike what you had thought you were cooking. Sometimes it's still edible. Other times, it's not.

Well, fortunately, the day I made these biscuits and this soup was definitely *not* one of those days.

The calendar said that a couple of weeks previously was the first day of spring, but the weekend I made this recipe was truly the first spring-like weather we'd had for more than five or ten minutes. Beautiful temperatures, sunny skies, light breezes. . . . It was a perfect day to Dutch oven.

Frankly, it was a perfect day to do anything outdoors.

At that time, I had been planning this tomato soup. I'd read what looked like a really good recipe, and I'd thought of some things that, in my mind, would really enhance it. The soup was to be made from scratch, as I tend to like doing. And by "scratch" I mean from tomatoes, not from a can. I'd been excited to try it. In fact, I'd pretty much decided that if I could pull it off, I would make it one of the first courses of my big Mother's Day dinner a few weeks afterward.

I'd also thought I'd do a sourdough bread to go with it, but then I thought of the time I would need to activate the starter and to do all the barm and sponge stuff. . . . I still wanted to do a bread, though, so I thought that I'd try some biscuits again. At that time, I'd had some real difficulty with biscuits (or any baking powder/soda–based leavened bread). I really needed to master it. I decided to try again that day.

Well, it all came together. A beautiful day, some magnificent biscuits, and possibly the best soup I'd ever tasted. And I decided that since it all ended up being so incredibly different from the original recipe, I'd claim it as my own! Man, what a day,

THE TOMATO SOUP

TOOLS

12-inch Dutch oven

20+ coals underneath to keep the soup boiling and then
simmering

INGREDIENTS

2 medium onions, chopped

2 Tbsp. minced garlic

2 Tbsp. oil/butter

6–7 medium tomatoes, peeled and chopped

4–5 cups chicken stock

3 sprigs celery, chopped

5–6 green onions, chopped (include some greens)

1 jalapeño, chopped

2 crumbled bay leaves

liberal shakes of (at start and occasionally during the cooking):

salt

coarse ground pepper

dried parsley

cumin

any other herb or spice you like

1–3 Tbsp. flour

FLAKY BISCUITS

TOOLS

12-inch Dutch oven

11–12 coals below

20–24 coals above

INGREDIENTS

4 cups flour

2 Tbsp. baking powder

2 tsp. salt

½ cup shortening

2 cups milk

more shortening

I started out by firing up a whole bunch of coals. Lots of them. I put the 12-inch Dutch oven over 18–20 coals and put in the first set of ingredients. I just let the onions and garlic cook to transparency.

Once they were getting done, I added all the second set of ingredients. I seasoned it at that point, and then again later on. It took quite a while for it to start boiling. I had to keep the lid on, although I didn't actually put any coals on the lid. I just kept it cooking and simmering while I made the biscuits.

The total cook time for the soup was somewhere around 2½–3 hours. After 1½ hours or so, I could see that the tomatoes had pretty much dissolved. Some of the other veggies were looking pretty frail too. I got a wire whisk and beat it through the mixture to blend it better and chop up any bigger veggie chunks. (If I'd had one of those hand blenders, I would've used that. You know, the ones with the cranks that spin a couple of blades around.)

After that, I let the soup simmer a while with the lid off. I had thought to cook it down some, but getting enough coals under the Dutch oven to keep it boiling without the lid on isn't easy.

With about 30 minutes to go, I added the flour. I actually added it with a fork so I could tap it and sprinkle it into the soup. Then I'd grab the whisk and blend it in. The flour thickened it up a bit, but not too much.

For the biscuits, I started by combining all of the dry ingredients, then added the shortening into that. With a pastry cutter, I mixed it all up and then added the milk.

When it was a nice, hefty dough, I pulled it out of the bowl and onto my floured countertop. I rolled it out and then folded it over. I kept doing that 5 or 6 times. Roll it out, fold it over. Sometimes I would flour in between folds. Those layers help to make the biscuits more flaky.

While I was doing all that, I put on some more coals. A lot of them, in fact. I was shooting for 400 degrees. Once the coals were white, I put them on and under the biscuit Dutch oven to preheat. I added some more shortening in the oven, which eventually melted, coating the bottom of the oven.

With the dough rolled out, I cut circles with a small drinking cup and then folded up and rerolled the dough, cutting more circles. Finally, I had cut all I could out of the dough, and I carried the dough rounds to the Dutch oven. The biscuit oven was now preheated.

I had decided to try a trick I'd read about. I set one of the biscuit dough rounds into the melted shortening in the Dutch oven. Then I turned it over and set it in place. Supposedly, the coated shortening would make for better browning. I did the same with all the dough discs, and then I set the Dutch oven lid with the coals back on the biscuits.

I baked the biscuits for about 30 minutes, turning the Dutch oven every 10 minutes or so. The biscuits were light, fluffy, and raised up. This was the first time I'd done biscuits that worked that well.

So the night's meal was a big success. The biscuits were fluffy and the soup was all *wow* and zesty. *Yummmm.*

And, I realized that with only a couple of ingredient changes, the meal could have been completely vegetarian if I'd used veggie stock (or even water) instead of chicken stock.

THESE LAST two recipes are named "breads" but end up being more like cakes. What's the difference between breads and cakes? Not much, really. They're both made with similar core ingredients: flour, water, sugar, leavening, eggs. I don't know why we call one a "bread" and the other a "cake."

Maybe it's the frosting.

Banana Nut Bread Supreme

I made this as the final course (dessert) in one of my seven-course Mother's Day feasts. It was a delicious end to a wonderful day. The drizzles at the recipe's end take it from simple to elegant!

TOOLS

12-inch Dutch oven

8–10 coals below

15–18 coals above

8-inch Dutch oven

7–9 coals below

INGREDIENTS

5 large ripe bananas

4 eggs, well beaten

1 cup shortening

2 cups sugar

4 cups flour

2 tsp. baking soda

1 tsp. baking powder

1 tsp. salt

1 cup chopped nuts (walnuts, almonds, or whatever)

2 bars of chocolate, chopped

1 cup butter

1 cup sugar

1–2 Tbsp. cinnamon

chocolate syrup

caramel syrup

whipped cream

I started by pureeing the bananas, and then I added the eggs. Some people say that you should eschew powered appliances when cooking in a Dutch oven. In fact, in many cook-offs, powered appliances aren't allowed. Usually I don't use them myself, preferring to do it by hand. But I decided to use the blender on the bananas. May the gods of cast iron forgive me. I got over it really fast though.

I put the shortening and the sugar in a bowl. I got out my pastry cutter and started cutting them together. It didn't take long to mix. Then I added the rest of the ingredients from the first set and mixed those together. So far, so good. I chose almonds because my wife and walnuts don't mix. And I chose good chocolate for an extra special taste.

Next I poured in the banana/egg mixture and stirred everything together.

I oiled and floured the bottom and sides of my Dutch oven and poured in the mix.

Somewhere in the process of making everything, I had lit my coals and set a lot of hot coals on the lid to preheat it. When the batter was ready, so was the lid. I put the lid on and baked for 45–60 minutes. I tested its doneness by sticking a fork in it. If the fork comes out clean, then the bread is done.

After I pulled the bread out of the Dutch oven and cooled it, I wrapped it in plastic so it wouldn't dry out.

At this point, it's a good banana bread. But I had to take it to another level. This was to be a fancy dinner, and it needed a fancy ending for that final "Wow!"

So right before serving the dessert, I slipped away from the dinner. In my 8-inch Dutch oven, I melted the butter, dissolved the sugar, and added the cinnamon. I came back in and sliced the banana bread into cake-like wedges. I scooped up some of the cinnamon butter sauce and put that in the bottom of a shallow bowl, and I added the cake on top of that. Then I drizzled the top of the cake with the chocolate and caramel syrups, making sure to get some drizzled on the bowl too. Finally, a *squirrch* of whipped cream on top and the dessert was onto the table.

The little bit of cinnamon and the syrups, combined with the whipped cream, was simple. But it took the dessert to another level.

Corn Bread Cake

My favorite way of making corn bread cake in the past was to make a corn bread mix, make a yellow cake mix, and then stir the two together. I thought there would be a way to make both of these from scratch, so I did some research and came up with this recipe. It ended up kind of like a cake with a bit of corn flavor.

Or was it corn bread, with a bit of lightness and moistness?

TOOLS

10-inch Dutch oven

9–10 coals below

18–20 coals above

INGREDIENTS

¼ cup butter, softened (the softer the better)

1 cup white sugar

3 eggs

1 cup cornmeal

2¼ cups all-purpose flour

1½ Tbsp. baking powder

1 tsp. salt

light shakes of cinnamon and nutmeg

½ cup vegetable oil

1 Tbsp. honey

1¾ cups whole milk

I started by lighting up the coals. Once these are white-edged, a lot of them will go on the Dutch oven lid to preheat it.

I creamed the butter and sugar together. I used the back of a big serving spoon to whip the two together and to incorporate as much air as possible. I did this for several minutes, until the mixture is nice and fluffy.

Then I added in the eggs, one at a time, beating and blending as I went. By this time, my arm was quite tired, and I took a break. I mixed the dry ingredients together into one bowl. In another bowl I mixed the remaining wet ingredients. After all this, I went out and put the coals on the lid, as I mentioned before.

Then I added half of the dry ingredients to the butter/sugar/egg mixture, and continued mixing, and then half of the wet, and mixed some more. While still mixing, I added the remainder of each. At that point it turned into a nice batter, which I finished mixing with a wire whisk to break apart the dry clumps.

I cut out a circle of parchment paper to line the bottom of the Dutch oven, even though I wasn't sure that I'd need it. I planned on serving cut squares directly from the Dutch, so I wouldn't need to flip it out like a cake. Still, I went with the parchment paper. I sprayed the sides of the Dutch oven with oil as well.

I poured in the batter, then put the heated lid on the Dutch oven. I counted out the proper coals above and below and set it to bake. I rotated the Dutch oven after about 15 minutes. After about 35 minutes, the cake was done! I brought it in and let it cool.

It was delicious, and it serves up well next to chili.

Conclusion

WOW. YOU'VE come a long way! If you've gone through this book cover to cover, I'll bet you've made some impressive loaves of bread. You probably have made a few flops too, but that's okay because it's all a part of learning.

I started baking with fear and trembling. My early failures both cut me down and fueled my desire to learn. It's my hope that with this book, your learning curve will be a little less steep. I hope you've had as much fun reading this book and trying the recipes in it as I had writing it.

Remember that there are many ways to do everything, and I've merely been sharing the methods I've learned. Even the writing of this book, with the additional discussion and research done, has taught me many more skills.

You and I, we'll always keep learning. We'll keep finding new tricks, new techniques, new recipes, and new ideas. I'll share mine at the blog: marks-blackpot.com. I hope you'll join me there and share yours too!

Until then . . .

Welcome to the 2 percent!

Resources

WEBSITES

- **Marksblackpot.com:** I constantly update my blog with more and more Dutch oven recipes. Meats, soups, stews, breads, desserts—I do them all. Come visit and try some. Leave a comment or a recipe of your own.

- **Spreadthebread.org:** This site is all about getting folks together to bake bread and share it with those in need. Really, when you think of basic, person-to-person charity, you can't get much more pure than this, can you?

- **Thefreshloaf.com:** This site is a social place for those who want to learn breadmaking from each other. Members post recipes, photos, processes, tips, and tricks. Of course, this site is about baking indoors, in a traditional oven, not outdoors in a Dutch oven. Still, there's a lot of great stuff to learn here.

- **Sodabread.info:** This is one of the sites I went to when I tried to learn how to do soda bread. Whoever owns this site is on a crusade to share good traditional soda bread with anyone who will listen and eat.

- **Sourdoughhome.com:** This site was also great resource to me when I was learning to make sourdough loaves. Lots of great information!

- **Idos.org:** For anyone who loves to Dutch oven, the International Dutch Oven Society is the club to join. You can find chapters all over the US and even a few in other countries. IDOS encourages cook-offs, demos, and Dutch oven gatherings for lots of face-to-face friendly cooking!

BOOKS

- *The Bread Baker's Apprentice: Mastering the Art of Extraordinary Bread* by Peter Reinhart

- *The Baking Book* by Lloyd Moxon

- *The Art of Bread* by Eric Treuille and Ursula Ferrigno

- *Artisan Bread in Five Minutes a Day: The Discovery That Revolutionizes Home Baking* by Jeff Hertzberg and Zoe Francois

Acknowledgments

MANY, MANY thanks:

To my dear wife, Jodi, who mocks me for my pickiness but loves the results! Mostly, thanks to her for her patience as I've written and promoted these books.

To my sons, Brendon and Jacob, who encourage me and try the things I cook and bake. They cook alongside me and are constant sources of clever ideas.

To my sister, Ruth, who was a great influence and resource to me as I struggled to work out the errors in my failures and who was the first to taste my success at my first bread party.

To my mom and my dad. To Mom for teaching me that there's more to bread than the airy fluff that's on America's supermarket shelves. She raised me on the whole-wheat recipe that's found in chapter four. To Dad for eagerly gobbling up all of the various breads Mom made, showing appreciation for her skills and variety.

To my friends at the International Dutch Oven Society, who have helped me and encouraged me as I've blogged and authored these books. What a great bunch! They are great chefs and wonderfully helpful people.

To Cedar Fort Publishing and all the wonderful people there for making these books possible!

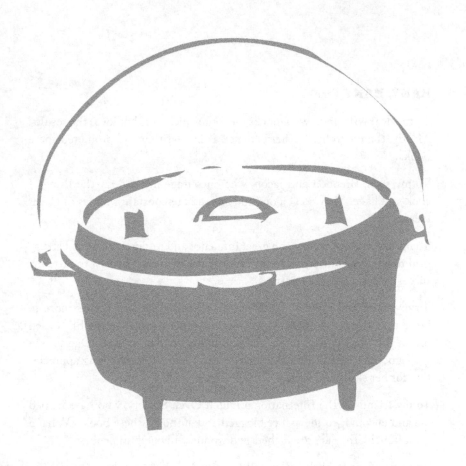

Index

T

V

W

Y

About the Author

MARK HANSEN started cooking in his Dutch ovens in 2006 when his wife surprised him with one as a Father's Day present. His first cooking attempt was pizza, and the family instantly declared it a success! He began a tradition of cooking the family's Sunday dinners in his Dutch ovens.

In April of the following year, he thought he should start sharing what he learned, and he established marksblackpot.com. Years and hundreds of recipes later, it's still one of the most widely read Dutch oven blogs on the Internet.

Mark lives in Eagle Mountain, Utah, with his wife, Jodi, and two boys, who are also budding chefs.

OTHER DUTCH OVEN BOOKS BY MARK HANSEN:

Best of the Black Pot

Black Pot for Beginners

Around the World in a Dutch Oven